Riva Castleman
is Deputy Director for Curatorial Affairs
and Director of the Department of Prints and Illustrated
Books at the Museum of Modern Art, New York. She joined
the Department of Drawings and Prints at the Museum of
Modern Art in 1963, and since then has been directly involved
in most of the Museum's exhibitions of prints and illustrated
books. Her other publications include *American Impressions:
Prints Since Pollock*, *Contemporary Prints*, *Printed Art*, *Prints
from Blocks* and monographs on
Jasper Johns and Matisse.

WORLD OF ART

This famous series
provides the widest available
range of illustrated books on art in all its aspects.
If you would like to receive a complete list
of titles in print please write to:

THAMES AND HUDSON
30 Bloomsbury Street, London WC1B 3QP
In the United States please write to:
THAMES AND HUDSON INC.
500 Fifth Avenue, New York, New York 10110

1 Pablo Picasso (1881–1973), *The Frugal Repast*, 1904; printed 1913. Etching, 18 $\frac{3}{16}$ × 14 $\frac{13}{16}$ (46 × 37·6). Gift of Abby Aldrich Rockefeller

RIVA CASTLEMAN

PRINTS
OF THE TWENTIETH CENTURY

Revised and enlarged edition

195 illustrations, 33 in color

THAMES AND HUDSON

All the illustrations in this book are from the collection
of The Museum of Modern Art, New York.

Published in the United States in 1988 by
Thames and Hudson Inc., 500 Fifth Avenue,
New York, New York 10110

Library of Congress Catalog Card Number 87-51289

Printed and bound in Spain by Artes Graficas Toledo S.A.
D.L.TO – 1401–1988

Traditions are beautiful – to create – not to follow

Franz Marc, 1915

Translated by Alfred H. Barr, Jr., in 1963 from
Franz Marc, *Briefe, Aufzeichnungen und Aphorism.*
Berlin, Paul Cassirer, 1920, p. 127

Contents

PHOTO CREDITS

1 Introduction: some nineteenth-century influences

IT HAS BECOME TRADITIONAL to begin a history of art of the twentieth century by discussing the various movements of the last decades of the nineteenth. However, one must view many ideas developed in the last century as continuing, but constantly being altered by subsequent twentieth-century ideas and attitudes. The historical process is such that unexpected discoveries occur only to those who are prepared: for Braque and Picasso it was how Cézanne's paintings appeared to them in 1907 that impelled them toward Cubism, not how Cézanne painted in the 1880s. A continuum of development that shaped their minds prepared them to accept this influence over others.

In the accelerated momentum that has characterized our own century, a remarkable artistic legacy has developed. The history of prints during the past eight and one half decades parallels that of other media. How different this century is from the last is found in the necessity now to refer to unique art and multiple art as genre terms; since the advent of collage in 1912 the terms 'painting' and 'sculpture' are no longer sufficiently inclusive. The printmaking media have also become more diversified as photographic techniques have been introduced and accepted. Because of economic and technological considerations there is usually a time lag between the appearance of new stylistic developments in unique media and their evolvement in prints. Few artists have been able to use the print media to inaugurate esthetic concepts. However, there is no question that these concepts have been modified and extended through the processes of printmaking.

Those artists who were primarily concerned with making unique works of art turned to printmaking during the nineteenth and twentieth centuries for various reasons. Gifted entrepreneurs, convinced of the esthetic value of an artist's work, have played a dominant role in

9

the translation of that quality into economic value. Most had little success at first, but without the tenacity of these visionaries the acceptance of prints as significant art would not have occurred. Without the aid of such astute (but not always financially successful) patrons, few young artists whose primary struggle was to paint or sculpt would have felt the need to create prints. An outstanding example of this situation is Pablo Picasso's second attempt at etching, *The Frugal*
I *Repast.* Encouraged by his friend Ricardo Canals, a printmaker from Barcelona, Picasso took a large secondhand plate and etched into it a variation on a theme that had first concerned him three years before: a couple seated at a café table. As it turned out, the etched conception was superior to many of the painted ones, but as Picasso's audience was limited in 1904, no one would undertake the printing of a large edition. Most of the first examples printed by Eugène Delâtre, a particularly knowledgeable etching and aquatint printer, were given by Picasso to his friends. The example illustrated here is from the edition of 250 commissioned in 1913 by France's foremost print and illustrated book impresario during the first four decades of this century, Ambroise Vollard. Vollard's gifts were showmanship and undertaking impossible tasks. He was nearly blind to the important strides toward abstraction that Picasso was making, and it was after the publicity given to the Cubist Picasso that Vollard issued his earlier, more generally palatable, prints. Picasso's Cubist prints, commissioned by Daniel H. Kahnweiler, were almost unsalable when issued.

The technological problems that surround an artist's entry into printmaking are considerable. If making prints has never been an integral part of an artist's creative life, to begin requires, at the very least, leaving the personal, isolated environment of the studio. Few artists have had, as Picasso did, the dazzling ability to perform what made his appearance in a printing shop an inspiration to all who surrounded him, who in turn stimulated him to even more and finer work. Artists have continued to make prints in their studios, particularly if they subscribe to creative philosophies that require either continuous direct involvement with materials or with folk-craft traditions. While the quantity of images created in the studio can be large, the number of each edition printed is determined most often by the amount of time the artist feels worthwhile spending on a labor of less than primary creative value. The variety of effects within such editions, since they come directly from the artist's hand, is one of the qualities lost in the larger printer's shop. As will be seen, the Expressionists in Germany felt that the making of prints was fundamental in representing their esthetic and consequently used print technology at its most unsophisticated and variable level.

The subject of uniform versus variable editions of prints becomes an important part of the history of twentieth-century printmaking. As more purely mechanical procedures have been introduced into the various techniques, an argument has developed that has created two persevering points of view. The technological revolution that characterizes this century has been accepted as beneficial and been exploited by the one camp. Personal gesture and 'feel' for materials, however, continue to represent significant factors to those who see prints in the same creative arena as painting and drawing. The two essentially diverging points of view continue to coexist in the last half of this century. (One might also study them in terms of action and reaction.) The advantage to artists who can avail themselves of the technically proficient workshop (albeit basically nineteenth century in structure) is that more of their works may be printed and therefore more widely distributed. In both cases, however, neither manual nor mechanical manufacture can destroy a good concept or redeem a poor one. It is the compatibility of technique and concept that has characterized quality in creative works, whatever the medium.

The following survey of art as it developed in the print media during the twentieth century is oriented toward historical analysis and away from technical dissection. Descriptions of printmaking methods appear only in the context of esthetic developments, as they reflect an artist's philosophical concerns or society's requirements. The surge in popularity of prints during the last decade of the nineteenth century established conditions that have encouraged almost every major twentieth-century artist to create prints. This circumstance allows a more complete review of the history of art of this period through prints than is possible for any previous century.

Some of the most significant prints of the twentieth century were made to illustrate books. This is particularly the case in Paris, where the *livre illustré* or *livre du peintre* was developed into an important form. While a suitable match of artist and writer was generally judged by the publisher to be basic to the successful outcome of his venture, such special conjunctions were often troublesome. It became far simpler to deal with only the artist, so texts by Virgil, Ovid, La Fontaine,

Balzac, and other writers well in their graves became the norm. As the illustrated book evolved in the late 1920s, its pictorial matter became more conspicuous. Extra suites of plates were added to special copies of the books, and many found their separate ways into the single print market. One could not have a thorough understanding of the prints of Picasso, Chagall, or Rouault without consulting those made as book illustrations. It would be impossible to study the printed works of the Fauves and the Cubists, much less those of the Surrealists, without delving into these special books.

While the production of the *livre illustré* occurred largely in France and became an increasingly more luxurious and consequently more conservative form, one cannot ignore the myriad of printed images that were created for books elsewhere. As the perimeters of that art form known as printmaking have widened to include new media, much of this expansion occurred in works created in conjunction with literature. No longer confined to strictly commercial usage, the stencil became a viable tool for artists through its imaginative utilization in the illustration of books. Photo-offset processes have most recently emerged among the media selected by artists for printmaking, and a substantial number of their works made by these processes first appeared in books.

Although the years between World War II and the late 1980s have been the most productive in the area of this study, the durability of works of this century's final half is still a matter of opinion. Contemporary values and points of view insistently color and shade any historical analysis. If they are taken in the context of the times in which they were written, critiques of contemporary and often radically advanced art, formerly respected but now out of favor, are again respectable. It is hoped that this premature attempt to put the twentieth-century artist's prints in historical perspective will also be permitted the charity of being viewed as a modest document of its time.

MOST OF THE ELEMENTS that characterized art of the 1890s were carried over into the early 1900s. While artistic involvement in printmaking did not stop abruptly and begin anew, there appears to have been a hiatus in French production after some exceptionally glorious years. The albums that contained the exquisite color lithographs of Henri de Toulouse-Lautrec, Pierre Bonnard and Edouard Vuillard were issued by 1899. The publishers of ambitious collections such as *L'Estampe*

SÉGUIDILLE.

Brune encore non eue,
Je te veux prefque nue
Sur un canapé noir
Dans un jaune boudoir,
Comme en mil huit cent trente.

Prefque nue et non nue
A travers une nue
De dentelles montrant
Ta chair où va courant
Ma bouche délirante.

27

2 Pierre Bonnard (1867–1947),
page 27 from *Parallèlement* by
Paul Verlaine. Paris, Vollard,
1900. Lithograph, page $11\frac{5}{8} \times 9\frac{1}{2}$
(29.5×24). Louis E. Stern
Collection

Originale, La Revue Blanche, and *L'Album des Peintres-Graveurs* either discontinued their programs or found it difficult to sell or to compile further albums of equal grandeur. Vollard had begun to introduce his artists to the art of book illustration, and the milepost that marks the beginning of the twentieth century is his publication in 1900 of Paul Verlaine's *Parallèlement* with 108 enchanting illustrations by Pierre Bonnard. Bonnard's prints in *Parallèlement*, unlike many of his earlier   2 lithographs of patchwork-like color and pattern, were linear crayon lithographs. This simple manner, which emphasized the evocative value of line, was refined to a rare degree of purity a few years later in the drawings and prints of Henri Matisse.

In Germany as in Paris the creative mood of the 1890s was pervasive. Edvard Munch, the Norwegian artist who produced most of his prints in Paris and Berlin, continued his personal and intensely emotional style into the 1900s. However, only a few twentieth-century prints by this artist have the passion and quality of his 1890s lithographs

3 Edvard Munch (1863–1944),
The Kiss, 1897–1902. Woodcut,
$18\frac{3}{8} \times 18\frac{5}{16}$ (46·7 × 46·5). Gift of
Abby Aldrich Rockefeller

4 (*below*) Max Klinger (1857–
1920), *The Plague*, 1903.
Etching, $19\frac{7}{16} \times 13\frac{3}{8}$ (49·3 × 34).
Purchase Fund

5 (*right*) Paul Klee (1879–1940),
Virgin in a Tree, 1903. Etching,
$9\frac{5}{16} \times 11\frac{11}{16}$ (23·6 × 29·7).
Purchase Fund

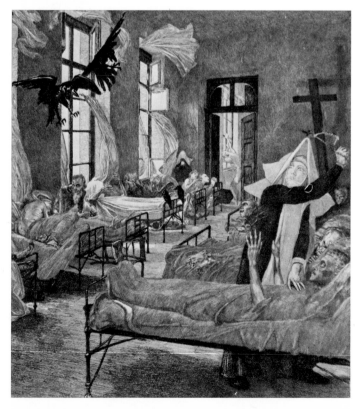

and woodcuts. The end of a love affair in 1902 began a difficult period for Munch, which culminated in his most severe nervous breakdown, in 1908. Munch began to carve his woodcut *The Kiss* in 1897 and re-   3 vised the entire relationship of the monolithic lovers to their background in 1902. The ruggedly simple central shape would be echoed in the work of the young German artists of Die Brücke in 1908.

From the nineteenth century also came a strong current of fantasy that had a determined moralizing tone. Both Munch and the Munich Symbolist Franz von Stuck (at whose academy Paul Klee was to study in 1900) depicted voluptuous ladies and titled them *Sin*. A hint of doomsday was never absent from the Belgian James Ensor's work, and a romanticized form of fatalism became a peculiarity of the Munich school. Max Klinger created several series of etchings in the 1880s and 1890s that visually presented the dream fantasies that Sigmund Freud was to explain shortly thereafter. Klinger's *The Plague* of 1903 repre-   4 sents the continuance of this tradition, which was to serve as a stepping-stone toward the metaphysically oriented works of de Chirico and Max Ernst.

At the moment of Klinger's *Plague*, however, the young seemed more concerned with minutely examining glaring truths about the

human condition. Twenty-three-year-old Picasso accentuated the miserable nature of the poor and blind through exaggeration of proportion and light in *The Frugal Repast*. Twenty-four-year-old Paul
5 Klee's *Virgin in a Tree* has a curious relationship to the grotesque political caricature of the time, but formal elements similar to those used by Picasso characterize this youthful yet highly professional early work. The element of satire was basic to a great deal of Germanic art, and Klee was to prove himself its most imaginative exponent.

The gently barbed humor of the French, particularly as it had found its pictorial form in the cartoons of Honoré Daumier, led to a different sort of expression. Jacques Villon found his first job as a cartoonist for several of the humorous publications that were favored by a segment of Parisian society. His excellent skill as a printmaker, learned from his uncle, was soon put to good use depicting children and beautifully coiffed and hatted ladies. Although Villon's interest seemed to lie solely in depicting the bourgeois society of his time, he was unable to refrain altogether from allowing vestiges of his past associations with French humor to enter his compositions. *The Game of Solitaire* is a
42 deft reflection of the trifling pastimes of the idle – the sweet irony of the woman *déshabillée* but still wearing her stylish hat! While Paul Helleu, James Tissot, and many others (including Villon himself) were executing charming 'Gibson Girl' drypoints, this color aquatint, which so astutely combines formal elements borrowed from the Nabis with the exaggeration of youthful expression, is another herald of twentieth-century developments.

Two nutrient streams of representation flowed into the twentieth century, one romantic and expressionist, the other classical and harmonious. In France the Fauves and in Germany members of Die Brücke and Der Blaue Reiter were nurtured on the emotive and expressive forms of late nineteenth-century art. Because the Germans saw their movement in terms of their already mentioned propensity toward moralizing and satire, they issued statements articulating their motivations. They derived an impetus toward printmaking from Munch, the precursor of Expressionism who made quantities of prints, and from their interest in primitive and folk wood-carvings. The French had to deal with the less pervasive influences of van Gogh and Gauguin. Their stronger direction was to be toward classicism, and this was to find its first form in Cubism.

2 Expressionism in France and Germany up to World War I: Fauves, Die Brücke, Der Blaue Reiter

HENRI MATISSE, Georges Rouault, Maurice de Vlaminck, André Derain, and Raoul Dufy were the main French artists to create prints in the Expressionist manner. These Fauves ('wild beasts', a name attached somewhat derisively to the group whose paintings were exhibited together in 1905 and 1906) were in revolt against the introverted eclecticism that restrained the vigorous development of Gauguin's and van Gogh's ideas. Violent color used independent of its normal descriptive role characterized their paintings. As did the German Expressionists, most of them preferred to use the gouge and woodblock as a means of conveying the energy that symbolized their revolt.

Georges Rouault has generally been treated as a unique stylist, but the character of his art developed directly out of the Fauve period. Although he did not work extensively in print media until 1916, he did execute his *Clown and Monkey* in 1910, which shows his Expressionist handling of color and surface. It is one of the few examples of prints in color by French artists who had been among the Fauves. More typical is Henri Matisse's lively *Nude Study* of 1906. Here the black line literally jolts the eye as it moves from the distorted figure to the waves of energy that activate the background while flattening perspective. It is as if the sinuous, languid patterns that typified the turn of the century had been given a shock treatment; the madly swirling brush strokes of van Gogh now became detached from the depiction of a state of nature. Matisse explained his attitude: 'Expression to my way of thinking does not consist of the passion mirrored upon a human face or betrayed by a violent gesture. The whole arrangement of my picture is expressive.'[1]

After more than a decade in which the color print (lithograph and aquatint) was brought to extreme refinement in Paris, it was inevitable that the newest ideas would find their printed form in black and white.

44

6

17

Picasso was not to make a multicolor print until 1939, and although a proof of *The Frugal Repast* and some of his small early woodcuts were printed in color, they were monochromatic. His *Head of a Young Woman* of 1906 (printed only once then, and in an edition in 1933) is one of the few instances in his work of the period that revealed his loose attachment to the ideas of the Fauves. This print as well as many of his drawings and paintings that led to *Les Demoiselles d'Avignon* (1907) were inspired by primitive carvings from Spain (Iberian stones from Osuna). He was to find masks and other sculpture from black Africa of even greater inspiration, and almost a decade later was to be characterized as 'The Bird of Benin' in Guillaume Apollinaire's novel *Le Poète Assassiné*.

Apollinaire was the major critic of the new art of the twentieth century as well as a close friend of many of the most gifted artists. He particularly admired André Derain, whom he chose to illustrate the first book he had published in Paris, *L'Enchanteur Pourrissant* (Kahnweiler, 1909). Derain's woodcuts, more decorative than narrative, epitomize the Fauve manner. Before this time Gauguin used the gouge

6 Henri Matisse (1869–1954), *Nude Study*, 1906. Woodcut, 18¾ × 15 (47·6 × 38). Gift of Mr. and Mrs. Kirk Askew, Jr.

7 Pablo Picasso (1881–1973), *Head of a Young Woman*, 1906; printed 1933. Woodcut, 20¼ × 13½ (51·4 × 34·3). Abby Aldrich Rockefeller Fund

to pick out his nudes from an exotic setting detailed by scratches and seemingly haphazard cutting, and Edouard Vallotton had no equal in balancing the areas of black and white in his woodcuts. Derain, using elements from both artists, created an overall pattern of black and white in which the forms that fulfill the function of creating depth relate so intimately to the figure that they crowd themselves and the striding nude flat up against the picture plane.

Another artist, among the Fauves early in his career, who collaborated with Apollinaire was Raoul Dufy. His illustrations for Apollinaire's *Le Bestiare ou Cortège d'Orphée* (Paris, Deplanche, 1911) were in an allover style similar to but more decorative than Derain's. Between 1910 and 1912 Dufy created a series of larger woodcuts, one of which, *Fishing*, shows how the revolutionary character of the Fauve woodcut became harmonious, the disturbing brutalizing cuts of Matisse now falling into regular rows and the contours of the bodies carefully shaped by parallel lines. This is almost a woodcut version of   *10*

8 André Derain (1880–1954), plate 2 from *L'Enchanteur Pourrissant* by Guillaume Apollinaire. Paris, Kahnweiler, 1909. Woodcut, page 10½ × 8 (26·6 × 20·3). Louis E. Stern Collection

9 Maurice de Vlaminck (1876–1958), *Head of a Girl*, c. 1906. Woodcut, 12⅜ × 9 (31·4 × 22·9). Gift of Abby Aldrich Rockefeller (by exchange)

10 Raoul Dufy (1877–1953), *Fishing*, 1912. Woodcut, 12 11/16 × 15 13/16 (32 × 40). Gift of Victor S. Riesenfeld

Divisionist painting, in which each stroke (cut or painted) is an object in the composition.

Maurice de Vlaminck was the last of the Fauves to have put into the woodblock the succinct expression of simplified form enlivened by the results of direct attack on a resistant material. The close friend of Derain, who had encouraged him to become an artist, Vlaminck was influenced more by the dynamism of van Gogh than the methodical exploration of either Derain or Matisse. His *Head of a Girl* – surely   9 executed around 1906, since Vlaminck fell under the spell of Cézanne's work in 1907 – is remarkable in its daring abstraction of physical form. This is not entirely due to distortion, but to the juxtaposition of known forms minimally defined. The irregular gouges in the background and on the model's dress disperse depth as well as create the passages of tone that balance the large white areas of face and neck.

The German artists were naturally closer to the influences of artists who had worked in their country. Although Munch had made prints in Paris, he continued to live most of each year in Germany. There was no single center of art, and so groups of artists would form and then disperse as the promise of teaching jobs or exhibitions called them elsewhere. Without the restrictions of a strong national art movement they were able to choose more freely among the influences of the past. Although they were vitally aware of the strength of French Post-Impressionism, they were also becoming more nationalistic. They searched out and vivified motifs and techniques that had been merely respected relics of the German cultural heritage. Simultaneously, they were at the center of a maelstrom of scientific exploration which opened up disturbing vistas within (Freud) and without (Einstein). They were inevitably bound to the social and political stresses that were to tear Central Europe apart. Their anxiety to create strong feelings of empathy is evident in the simplicity they chose for their compositions and the directness of their statements. Like the French, they were responsive to the primitive objects from Africa and Oceania that they found housed in ethnographic museums. The word 'expressionism' was French, not German, and it was well after the inception of the free, revolutionary style of Die Brücke that the term was applied to German art.

The group of four architectural students who in 1905 formed Die Brücke ('The Bridge') in Dresden were Ernst Ludwig Kirchner, Erich Heckel, Karl Schmidt-Rottluff, and Fritz Bleyl. In their manifesto written by Kirchner in 1906, they called 'upon all youth to unite' and 'create . . . a physical and spiritual freedom opposed to the values of the comfortably established older generation.'² Kirchner had learned linoleum-carving from Bleyl and had alternately studied architecture in Dresden and painting in Munich before the group was formed in his studio. In 1906 Schmidt-Rottluff encouraged Emil Nolde, a much older artist, to join. In 1910, when several members exhibited in Berlin with

11 Ernst Ludwig Kirchner (1880–1938), *Three Women Conversing*, 1907. Woodcut, 15¾ × 13⅝ (39 × 34·6). Gift of Abby Aldrich Rockefeller

12 Ernst Ludwig Kirchner (1880–1938), *Nude Dancers*, 1909. Woodcut, 14⅜ × 20⅞ (36·5 × 53). Purchase Fund

the Neue Sezession, they became acquainted with Otto Müller, who joined Die Brücke. Bleyl, who had not really participated in the program, returned to academic life in 1909. Nolde, essentially a solitary artist, remained a member for only one year. Müller's association lasted until the group dispersed shortly before World War I.

Two prints by Kirchner well illustrate the direction taken by Die Brücke. The color woodcut *Three Women Conversing* of 1906–07, with its large contoured masses, is part of that newer, more romantically inclined balance that was forecast in Munch's woodcut *The Kiss*. The German form of Art Nouveau continued to contribute to this revolution, but as the new group sought inspiration elsewhere, a synthesis of many styles took place. The black and white *Nude Dancers* of 1909 is more immediate and insistently balanced in an altogether fresh way. It is perhaps one of the few German prints that links the German and French Expressionist movements. Kirchner was to go on, typically incorporating primitive and avant-garde influences, to create hundreds of prints. His color woodcuts, made after he assimi-

11

12

lated the superficialities of Cubist and Futurist planar elements, are
particularly engaging.

The use of color in prints was basic to the expression of Die Brücke
and later groups. Printmaking was far better associated with their
daily creations – and the tradition far stronger – in Germany than in
France. The formation of organizations by the artists included facilities
for printmaking as well as exhibiting. Experimentation within this
community system allowed printmaking to exist at a more powerful
level than in France, and from the beginning color played a definite
role. Erich Heckel's *Franzi Reclining* of 1910 shows to what degree
color could be used in defining flattened space. The figure, simplified
and distorted, is a combination of sharp angles and sweeping curves
against an irregular rectangle given form by the black, slightly angled
ground. In other instances Heckel distorts the expected by the inclusion, in the Fauvist manner, of unnatural color. Perhaps the best
known of these works is his *Self Portrait* of 1919, in which he experimented with covering the face with various colors, particularly an
olive green.

Schmidt-Rottluff, the only other original member of Die Brücke
to make prints during its existence, introduced lithography to the
others. His portrait of Heckel of 1909 and Max Pechstein's portrait of

43

13, 14

13 (*far left*) Karl Schmidt-Rottluff
(1884–1976), *Erich Heckel*, 1909.
Lithograph, $15\frac{5}{8} \times 12\frac{5}{8}$ (39·6 × 32). James
Thrall Soby Fund

14 (*left*) Max Pechstein (1881–1955),
Erich Heckel I, 1908. Lithograph,
$17 \times 12\frac{15}{16}$ (43 × 32·8). Lent anonymously

15 Emil Nolde (Emil Hansen) (1867–
1956), *The Prophet*, 1912. Woodcut,
$12\frac{5}{8} \times 8\frac{7}{8}$ (32 × 22·5). Given anonymously

Heckel of the previous year are examples of the experimental manner
in which they approached lithography. While they appear technically
undisciplined or naïve, the effects are those that Kirchner, writing in
the third person of his own style, described carefully: 'His method of
etching with turpentine produced tonal effects on the stone which had
never been seen before. His lithos are all hand-printed. He works his
stones until the preparatory drawing has been made completely
graphic. That is, the drawn lines vanish and are formed anew by
etching. Deep blacks alternate with silky grays which are produced by
the grain of the stone. The soft tonality, resulting from the gray
portions distributed by the grain of the stone, functions as color and
gives warmth to the print. In this way Kirchner developed a personal
lithographic technique which is much richer than the woodcut.'[3] In
both prints the loose line and gray tones are quite unlike the precise
crayon-drawn lithographs of the past. Pechstein's head particularly
shows the emotionally motivated brush strokes of Expressionist
painting.

The foremost of the Expressionist lithographs, however, were
created by Emil Nolde. His association with Die Brücke was minimal,
but he did learn lithography and woodcutting with them. His woodcuts are a skillful blend of deep spirituality and technical mastery (he

16 Otto Müller (1874–1930), *Two Gypsy Girls in Living Room* from *Zigeunermappe*, 1927. Lithograph, 27½ × 19¾ (69·8 × 50). Gift of Herbert Ziebolz

17 Max Pechstein (1881–1955), *Dialogue*, 1920. Woodcut, 15$\frac{13}{16}$ × 12$\frac{9}{16}$ (40 × 32). Gift of Paul J. Sachs

15   had studied wood-carving during the 1880s). *The Prophet* of 1912 is a powerful example of what can be done with direct carving into a plank of wood, revealing a form, as in sculpture, without destroying the character of the material. Nolde's lithographs approached the brilliance of color characteristic of his watercolors and paintings. He demonstrated that there could be great freedom in that medium, and was continually fascinated with changing color combinations within
45   a single composition. In the lithograph *The Young Couple* of 1913, the slightly swaying figures that seem to be as related to Indonesian dancers as to northern Gothic mannerisms are enveloped in sheets of color. There were more than sixty-eight variations of colors in the printings of this composition, all brilliant and harsh contrasts: blue and green, red and pink, yellow and violet, and so on.

Otto Müller, the last artist to join Die Brücke, began his association in 1910 in Berlin when several of his new colleagues were exhibiting with the Neue Sezession. Pechstein was expelled from Die Brücke in 1912 for showing once again with the Neue Sezession after the group had decided against exhibiting. In 1913 Kirchner's *Chronicle of*

26

Die Brücke appeared, and the remnants of the group disbanded – because of disagreement with Kirchner's interpretation of their history, it has been said. Müller's prints, mostly lithographs, had as their dominant subject an idyllic scene of female nudes bathing in a tropical setting. The bathers' long torsos and short hair as well as the spiky foliage indicate Müller's interest in African motifs. His gestural crayon lines lend to his prints an animated atmosphere that counteracts some- what his narrow imagination. A portfolio of color lithographs *16* depicting gypsies (1927) was his most successful printed work.

The later prints by members of Die Brücke, executed after they had dispersed, were often laden with the diagonals and sharp angles that derived to some extent from Futurism and Cubism. At the end of World War I Kirchner suffered from psychological disturbances. In his retreat in the Swiss Alps he worked with compulsive energy, creating many jagged woodcuts. Among these is the haunting *Winter Moonlight* done in 1918. Because he did his own printing, Kirchner *49* controlled the overprintings of the now traditional unnatural color with considerable finesse. At almost the same moment Schmidt-Rottluff cut the very geometric *Landscape at Dangast* (1917). His wood- *18* cuts tended toward a systematic angularity which often created a stronger impression of folk art than of a compelling expression of passion. At about the same time as this unusually serene composition, he was also cutting a series of the Stations of the Cross in which his leaning toward a Christian primitive tradition manifests itself. He was

18 Karl Schmidt-Rottluff (1884–1976), *Landscape at Dangast*, 1917. Woodcut, $11\frac{1}{2} \times 13\frac{5}{16}$ (29·2 × 33·8). Gift of Mrs. Heinz Schultz

to outlive every other member of Die Brücke. Pechstein, whose work was the first to gain acceptance, created his best-known woodcut in
17 1920. The *Dialogue* is perhaps the most definitive work done by an early Expressionist that is motivated almost exclusively by the appearance of African sculpture. Unlike Schmidt-Rottluff, who executed many woodcuts in African style, Pechstein managed to integrate this element without entirely mimicking its superficial details.

There were several artists who, in their mature years, became caught up in the Expressionist movement. Christian Rohlfs was already almost sixty years old when he began to create woodcuts. He was artist in residence at Karl Ernst Osthaus's museum in Hagen (Folkwang Museum in Essen after 1923) until he was almost seventy, and it was there, in the midst of an extraordinary collection of van Gogh

19 Christian Rohlfs (1849–1938), *Two Dancers*, c. 1913. Woodcut, 11 × 11$\frac{15}{16}$ (28 × 30·3). Mathew T. Mellon Foundation Fund

20 Lovis Corinth (1858–1925), *Death and the Artist* from *Totentanz*. Berlin, Euphorion, 1921. Etching and drypoint, 9⅜ × 7 (23·8 × 17·8). Gift of J. B. Neumann

and Gauguin paintings, that he found the inspiration that was to give to his compositions a unique quality of expression. He made imaginative use of inks and paints when printing his woodblocks and stencils. The *Two Dancers*, which he cut around 1913 (later published in an edition in the fifth Bauhaus Portfolio in 1921), appears to derive both from early German woodcuts of the Dance of Death and from imagined movements of primitive ceremonies. *19*

Lovis Corinth, one of the most prolific printmakers of the twentieth century, was considered a major German Impressionist painter. His landscapes and narrative lithographs are generally placid, while many of the drypoints and etchings made after a serious illness around 1911 have some of the dramatic force of the best Expressionist art. He was part of the Sezession in Berlin, against which the members of Die Brücke joined with others in the Neue Sezession. The work of his late years consisted almost entirely of prints, and his compelling self portrait *Death and the Artist* (1921) is a merciless dissection of character. *20*

It seems to derive from an admiration of Rembrandt and a consciousness of the new objectivity (Neue Sachlichkeit) that had emerged among the disillusioned in war-torn Germany.

It was not simply the war that destroyed for many their idealism and complacency. Social struggle was ever present, and where the illnesses of society pressed insistently against those who preferred to ignore them, graphic images aided in the assault. Käthe Kollwitz was the wife of a doctor in the slums of Berlin. In her *Death and a Woman*
21 *Struggling for a Child* of 1911 the excruciating pain of the subject is expressed in rounded, classic form. Kollwitz had studied sculpture at the Académie Julian in Paris. She continued to create sculpture and prints of great emotional power into the 1930s, but her execution and compositional structure never had the gestural force of the Expressionists.

Ernst Barlach was a sculptor who used the imagery of northern Germany's peasant life, still medieval and laden with Christian

21 Käthe Kollwitz (1867–1945), *Death and a Woman Struggling for a Child*, 1911. Etching, 16⅛ × 16³⁄₁₆ (40·9 × 41·1). Gift of Mrs. Theodore Boettger

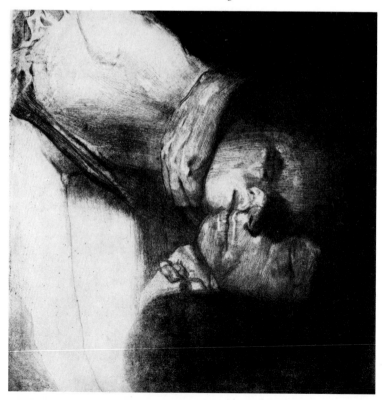

22 Ernst Barlach (1870–1938), *The First Day* from *Metamorphic Creations of God*. Berlin, Paul Cassirer, 1921. Woodcut, $10\frac{1}{8} \times 14\frac{1}{16}$ (25·7 × 36). Gift of Victor S. Riesenfeld

mysticism, as the basis of his unique contribution to Expressionist art. His work was almost entirely devoted to divulging a relationship between a higher being and man through a rugged and natural simplicity. He illustrated his and others' writings with many wood-cuts and lithographs. The seven woodcuts for his *Metamorphic Creations of God* (*Die Wandlungen Gottes*, 1921) are filled with the monumental power of his sculpture conveyed through figures that seem to be hewn from the solid rock of simple faith. Barlach was never allied to a specific Expressionist movement. He was convinced that 'the vulgar, universally human, primeval racial feelings . . . are great and timeless,'[4] and like Kollwitz, who was his good friend, he remained loyal to the human form as the container of the spiritual in art.

Having isolated the Expressionist tendencies of German artists, we can hardly continue their historical development without taking into account the evolution of Cubism and its related movements. At the time the exhibitions of the Neue Sezession were taking place in

Berlin, Munich was the site of two exhibitions of Picasso's paintings, in 1909 and 1911, and the exhibition of the Neue Künstlervereinigung, from which Der Blaue Reiter sprang, included Cubist works by both Picasso and Braque. The art of the Munich artists August Macke, Franz Marc, and Wassily Kandinsky merged the vigorous emotionalism that characterized the work of the Dresden and Berlin artists with the analytical exploration of form, color, and movement that was the basis for much of the new art throughout Europe. The German manifestation was, as is to be expected, more graphic than French Cubism or Italian Futurism. Thus, it is impossible to see the few Cubist prints as having had much influence on the woodcuts that continued to be produced by German-based artists.

Wassily Kandinsky had studied law in Moscow but turned to painting at the age of thirty. He studied in Munich and formed a group there, Phalanx, which was oriented toward Art Nouveau as well as Post-Impressionist French art. After participating in the Munich Sezession, he was instrumental in founding the Neue Künstlervereinigung, from which he broke in 1911. With Franz Marc and Gabriele Münter he formed the association Der Blaue Reiter. They envisioned and later published a periodical that reflected their ideas. As they brought together works and articles for the publication, they also organized two exhibitions. The second, during March–April 1912, was devoted exclusively to drawings and prints and included works by Die Brücke artists as well as Arp, Braque, Derain, Klee, Malevich, and Picasso. Probably for the first time outside of Kahnweiler's gallery in Paris, Picasso's earliest Cubist etchings (for Max Jacob's book *Saint Matorel*) were shown.

Marc discussed the exhibition in the *Almanach der Blaue Reiter* (Munich, R. Piper Verlag, 1912) and wrote about the 'savages' (the term equivalent to Fauves which he considered descriptive of himself and other German Expressionists): 'The young French and Russian artists who exhibited with them as guests had a liberating effect. They made one think. One came to understand that art was concerned with the deepest things, that a true revival could not be a matter of form but had to be a spiritual rebirth. *Mysticism* awoke in their souls and with it the primeval elements of art. . . . They have a different goal: to create *symbols* for their age, symbols for the altars of a new spiritual religion. The artist as a technician will simply vanish behind such works.' This mysticism, which Kandinsky clarified in his book

32

23 Wassily Kandinsky (1866–1944), plate 8 from *Klänge*. Munich, R. Piper, 1913. Woodcut, page $11\frac{1}{16} \times 11$ (28·3 × 28). Louis E. Stern Collection

Concerning the Spiritual in Art (1912), was a needed element in making art out of intellectual and emotional input.

Kandinsky decorated both his own book and the *Almanach der Blaue Reiter* with woodcuts, but his most cogent and encompassing Expressionist prints appeared in his book of poetry, *Klänge* (Munich, R. Piper Verlag, 1913). These images range from Russian folk art and Jugendstil motifs to purely abstract compositions that are some of the foundation blocks for one wing of truly twentieth-century art.

23

Throughout the stylistic changes in the illustrations there runs a naturalizing strain that links the abstract with a sense of life and the forms of reality.

Franz Marc's prints developed from the idyllic depiction of nature, particularly animals in natural settings, to dynamic abstract composi-
24 tions in which all elements are electrifyingly set into motion. Killed in the Battle of Verdun in 1916, he had only a few years to move from Fauve-like sensitivity to the synthesis of science and mysticism that functioned for him, as it did for Kandinsky, as the true foundation of reality. This allowed him to separate subject from realistic form, not only as Die Brücke artists did, by distortion and unnatural color, but by introducing compositional constructions that would expand the nature of experience and supersede empirical reality.

24 Franz Marc (1880–1916), *Riding School*, 1913. Woodcut, $10\frac{5}{8} \times 11\frac{3}{4}$ (27 × 29.8). Gift of Abby Aldrich Rockefeller

25 Wilhelm Lehmbruck (1881–1919), *Apparition*, 1914. Drypoint, $7 \times 9\frac{5}{16}$ (17·8 × 23·6). Gift of Samuel A. Berger

August Macke, who died in 1914, and Paul Klee were other members of Der Blaue Reiter who made prints. Macke's few woodcuts hardly reflect his exceptional gifts or his successful assimilation, in his paintings, of Robert Delaunay's color theories (Orphism). Klee, though not yet sure of his direction, appears to have acquired freedom from the belabored execution of his early etchings. Most of the early Expressionists made etchings or drypoints. Nolde's are the most assured, but they and those of Kirchner, Pechstein, and Schmidt-Rottluff have very little of the excitement generated by the woodcuts and lithographs of the same artists.

There was, during the early decades of this century, a now forgotten proliferation of sentimental but technically refined etchings. In reaction to these almost mechanically made commodities, many of the Expressionist artists sought to create effects of spontaneity upon their copper or zinc plates, allowing mistakes and foul bitten areas to remain

35

part of their compositions. It was not unusual for an artist such as the sculptor Wilhelm Lehmbruck to fill a plate with figure sketches in which each line from which the forms grew remains. Most of Lehmbruck's tenuous drypoints were created in Paris between 1910 and 1914 and, like the drypoints of the Cubists of the same period, have the quality of sketches wherein compositional problems are worked out directly. The trial proof of *Apparition* (1914) belonged to Heinrich Stinnes of Cologne, the first comprehensive collector of late nineteenth- and twentieth-century prints.

25

World War I was a major determinant in the future of all the artistic movements. Lehmbruck had to return to Germany at the beginning of hostilities. As has already been noted, several prominent German artists lost their lives in the war. Kandinsky and other Russian artists in both Germany and France went back to their homeland. In France the departure of many artists for army duty destroyed the continuity of their common creative goals. The deportation of German aliens and seizure of their property, as in the case of the art dealer and publisher D. H. Kahnweiler, ruptured the commerce of art. Of his comrade in the development of Cubism, Picasso remarked that after Braque left for the army, he never saw him again. While this was not actually the case, it was true that the two men never again shared the closely allied spirit that gave birth to the classical (as opposed to romantic) form of abstraction, Cubism.

3 Cubism and early abstract movements

DURING THE TIME that Expressionism expanded and matured in Germany it was intensely concerned with graphics. The flourishing of printmaking in the Expressionist movement was a positive contribution to a long tradition. Kirchner even based his inspiration on the actual appearance of Dürer's woodblocks, which he saw in Nuremberg. There was, in addition, the appeal of folk art, which intensified the tendency toward a craftsman-like approach to the making of art works and particularly prints. In contrast, the vital expansion of lithography in France during the 1890s was attached to a workshop situation involving printers and specialists. Whereas the members of Die Brücke, for example, worked together for a few years as a commune and shared their printing facilities, the artists in Paris were more independent, at least during their working periods. Even the least salable graphics were printed by professional printers in Paris.

It is no wonder that very few prints in the Analytical Cubist style developed by Braque and Picasso were printed during the period of the movement. The two artists devoted their energies to expanding a painterly mode which, having taken the work of Cézanne as a point of departure, was concerned with volume rather than line. There were, of course, attempts by the Cubists to translate the simultaneity of visual impressions of volume, which they depicted in shaded planes in their paintings, into linear form. Picasso attempted the first prints in this style in his illustrations for Max Jacob's book *Saint Matorel*, published by Kahnweiler in 1911.

Before executing the four etchings for *Saint Matorel* in the Catalan village of Cadaqués, where he spent the summer of 1910, Picasso made two small drypoints that begin to translate natural form into geometric form. Following the precepts of Cézanne, whose memorial retrospective in Paris in October 1907 was of momentous import to the

26 Pablo Picasso (1881–1973),
Two Nude Figures, 1909.
Drypoint, $5\frac{1}{8} \times 4\frac{15}{16}$ (13 × 11).
Purchase Fund

future Cubists, Picasso in 1909 composed human and still life alike 'in terms of the cylinder, the sphere, the cone, all seen in perspective, so that each side of an object or plane is directed toward a central point.'[5]

26 From the experimental drypoint *Two Nude Figures* to the plates of
27 *Saint Matorel* was a giant step in expanding Cézanne's formal concept. The compositions are built from a series of planes that are centrally attached to a frame of lines following the basic formal structure of the subject: a human body, still life, or building. The subject is centrally oriented and, as in his paintings, Picasso has allowed large areas of the rectangular composition to remain unembellished. This adherence to the classical formula for portraiture and figure representation exemplifies a fundamental difference between the Cubists and the work of the Fauves and other Expressionists who covered the picture plane as tightly as possible. In both cases, however, the artists were actively destroying the concept of the creation of an illusion of depth in their pictures. The idea of restricting the definition of form to bare

38

27 Pablo Picasso (1881–1973), plate 3 from *Saint Matorel* by Max Jacob. Paris, Kahnweiler, 1911. Drypoint, page 10½ × 8¾ (26·7 × 22·2). Louis E. Stern Collection

28 Pablo Picasso (1881–1973), *Still Life with Bottle*, 1912. Drypoint, $19\frac{11}{16} \times 12$ (50 × 30·5). Acquired through the Lillie P. Bliss Bequest

essentials, which was the abstracting tendency of the Expressionists, was carried into the realm of intellect by the Cubists. After defining the basic structure of their subjects, the Cubists examined simultaneously the natural direction of each component and as many aspects as possible of these components seen sequentially.

In 1911 and 1912 Picasso and Braque synthesized their increasingly complex, analytical pictorial approach by restricting their formerly simultaneous depiction of objects to one or two aspects only. This occurred most definitively with their collages in 1912. A series of planes almost entirely parallel to the picture plane was created, texture and color creating the effect of some visual sequence. At about the same moment they both executed drypoints that recorded the transition then taking place. In both drypoints the introduction of lettering establishes the frontal and direct relationship of the subject, a still life,

28, 29

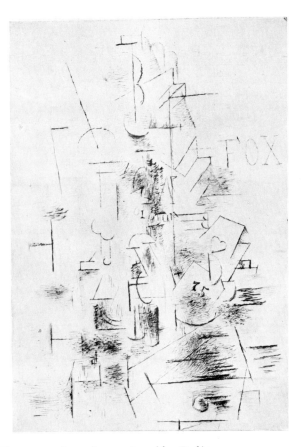

29 Georges Braque (1882–1963), *Fox*,
1912. Drypoint, $21\frac{1}{2} \times 15$ (54·6 × 38).
Purchase Fund

with the surface of the paper. These two drypoints, printed by Delâtre in 1912 for Kahnweiler, were published in editions of one hundred. One other drypoint by Braque was printed, and seven others were rejected by Kahnweiler. After the rejected plates were found by William S. Lieberman in 1948, they were published for the first time, in editions of fifty and thirty-five, by Aimé Maeght.

Picasso's primacy in the development of Cubism was known to very few. Except for the rare appearance of one of his Cubist paintings in Kahnweiler's gallery, Picasso remained for most the painter of acrobats. It was his colleague in Cubism, Braque, who had not enjoyed an earlier success as had Picasso, who showed his work and suffered the brunt of some of the critical outrage. (It was in Braque's early blocklike landscapes that Henri Matisse saw 'little cubes' and to which Louis Vauxcelles referred when he wrote in 1908, 'He is contemptuous of form, reduces everything, sites and figures and houses to geometric schemes, to cubes.'⁶) Although he occasionally sent a painting to the Salons, not even Braque was at the center of the movement as far as the public knew. It was the exhibition of a group of Cubists at the 1911 Salon des Indépendants that brought the new attitude toward objective painting to greater attention, and neither of its two initiators was included. Jean Metzinger, Albert Gleizes, Henri Le Fauconnier, Fernand Léger, and Robert Delaunay were allowed to show as a group, and Apollinaire labeled them 'Cubists' when they were invited to show in Brussels that June. In 1912 Gleizes and Metzinger, the first artists to explain this new art in their book *Du Cubisme* (1912), met with Jacques Villon at his studio in Puteaux and decided to show together in an exhibition they were to call *Section d'Or*. Most of the artists included in that exhibition worked according to some version of the Cubist formula. Villon, his brothers Marcel Duchamp and Raymond Duchamp-Villon, Francis Picabia, Juan Gris, Louis Marcoussis, Léger, Alexander Archipenko, André Dunoyer de Segonzac, and many others exhibited. For the most part they were more science-oriented and less instinctive than Picasso and Braque. There is less evidence, too, of the influence of primitive art.

It is at this point that we can again pick up the thread of printmaking, for Villon became the most prolific Cubist printmaker and Marcoussis executed one of the most important Cubist images in print. Villon, much older than his exhibiting colleagues, had worked in etching, as we have seen, for more than a dozen years. His distillation of the Cubist idiom was accomplished in easy stages, from his laconic

30   volumetric portrait *Renée, three-quarters view* (1911) to the planar
31   definition of his *Portrait of a Young Woman* and the nearly complete
32   abstraction of *The Dinner Table* (1913). He was to continue throughout his life to construct his compositions from the arcs, wedges and oblique geometric forms that he devised before World War I.

The Polish Louis Marcoussis, another artist who, like Villon, started out as a cartoonist and found etching as viable an expressive
33   medium as painting, began in 1912 a portrait of Guillaume Apollinaire which was completed in 1920. Because of its classic pattern of mounting oblong planes and its subject, the foremost explicator of Cubism, this etching and its unique earlier version (Arensburg Collection, Philadelphia Museum of Art) embody the essence of Cubist printmaking. In the hands of Villon and Marcoussis the Cubist-inspired

30 Jacques Villon (Gaston Duchamp) (1875–1963), *Renée, three-quarters view*, 1911. Drypoint, $21\frac{5}{8} \times 16\frac{5}{16}$ (55×41.4). Purchase Fund

31 Jacques Villon (Gaston Duchamp) (1875–1963), *Portrait of a Young Woman*, 1913. Drypoint, $21\frac{9}{16} \times 16\frac{1}{4}$ (54.7×41.3). Gift in memory of Peter H. Deitsch

32 Jacques Villon (Gaston Duchamp) (1875–1963), *The Dinner Table*, 1913. Drypoint, $11\frac{1}{8} \times 15$ (28.2×38). Purchase Fund

33 Louis Marcoussis (1883–1941), *Portrait of Guillaume Apollinaire*, 1912–20. Etching and drypoint, $19\frac{9}{16} \times 10\frac{15}{16}$ ($50 \times 27\cdot7$). Given anonymously.

34 Louis Marcoussis (1883–1941), *Still Life: Zither and Seashell*, 1922. Etching and aquatint, $20\frac{1}{2} \times 27\frac{7}{8}$ ($52 \times 70\cdot8$). Abby Aldrich Rockefeller Fund

35 Juan Gris (1887–1927), plate 2 from *Ne coupez pas Mademoiselle ou Les erreurs de P.T.T.* by Max Jacob. Paris, Galerie Simon, 1921. Lithograph, page $12\frac{1}{2} \times 8\frac{7}{8}$ ($31 \cdot 7 \times 22 \cdot 5$). Louis E. Stern Collection

print changed from an enigmatic linear rendering of a painterly idiom, as purveyed by Picasso and Braque, to a solid, geometricized depiction in balanced quantities of dark and light. As was to be expected, this refinement was to become more and more decorative. A synthetic etching and aquatint of sublime contrasts, Marcoussis's *Still Life: Zither and Seashell* (1922) is, however, a noble parent to geometrical abstraction. *34*

The war interrupted the flourishing of the Cubist idiom among French artists. Juan Gris, like Picasso a Spanish national, was able to continue painting in France during the war. He, too, was associated with Kahnweiler, and while he made few attempts at printmaking in his short lifetime, he did illustrate several books. His lithographs for *Ne coupez pas Mademoiselle* (Galerie Simon, 1921), a poem in collage style by Max Jacob, are simplified and more readable than his prewar paintings. They are true illustrations, referring directly to the text.[7] The showcard lettering and flowery script which identify the illustration are also important compositional forms. *35*

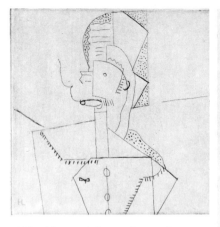

36 Henri Laurens (1885–1954), cover from
Les Pélican by Raymond Radiguet. Paris,
Galerie Simon, 1921. Etching, page 12¾ ×
8¹⁵⁄₁₆ (32·4 × 22·7). Louis E. Stern Collection

37 Robert Delaunay (1885–1941), *The Eiffel
Tower*, 1926. Transfer lithograph, 24¼ × 17¾
(61·6 × 45). Purchase Fund

Most Cubist-manner sculpture was executed quite late in the period
of Cubism's development. Much of it was created by foreigners in
Paris (Archipenko, Jacques Lipchitz, Max Weber), but Henri Laurens,
deferred from military duty, was the only Frenchman who devoted
his main energies to developing the Cubist idiom in sculpture. His
36   etchings for Raymond Radiguet's book *Les Pélican* (Galerie Simon,
1921), though quite simply linear, allude to the sense of dimensional
movement in Laurens's sculpture.

While his few prints are composed after specific paintings and done
sixteen years after them, Robert Delaunay's lithographs of buildings
are among the most vital Cubist graphics. After the early proto-
Cubist landscapes, the subjects which the Cubist artists preferred for
their compositions were still lifes and figures (generally three-
quarters and seated). The transfer lithograph of *The Eiffel Tower*
37   (1926, after the paintings of 1910–11) is solely in black and white,
clearly exposing the raw bones of Delaunay's fragmented approach.
After 1911 Delaunay moved very quickly away from the dynamic

46

vision of *The Eiffel Tower* to a purely abstract concept of simultaneous color relationships, which Apollinaire named 'Orphism.'

Elsewhere, the effects of Delaunay's surging apocalyptic compositions helped to inspire two American-born artists, John Marin and Lyonel Feininger. Marin had been in Europe between 1905 and 1911 and was not only familiar with the artistic developments in Paris but was a member of Alfred Stieglitz's gallery in New York, where Picasso's Cubist work was seen before most of Paris knew about it. Marin's *Woolworth Building (The Dance)* (1913) combines etching with   *38* staccato drypoint, less solid in its Cubist structure than the French idiom and more allied to the usage made of Cubist effects by Der Blaue Reiter. Feininger spent most of his life in Germany, first working as a cartoonist. Between 1906 and 1908 he used his whimsical imagination on the Parisian scene. He was intrigued by the work of his acquaintance Delaunay when he saw it during a visit to Paris in 1911 and made use of the new ideas. While Franz Marc went in the same coloristic direction as Delaunay after seeing the latter's work in Paris in 1912, Feininger was clearly more interested in intersection and fragmentation of planes in his etching and drypoint *The Gate*   *39* (1912). Like Marin he contrasts the strength, size, and vibrancy of

38 John Marin (1870–1953), *Woolworth Building (The Dance)*, 1913. Etching, $13\frac{1}{16} \times 10\frac{5}{8}$ (33 × 27). Edward M. M. Warburg Fund

39 Lyonel Feininger (1871–1956), *The Gate*, 1912. Etching and drypoint, $10\frac{11}{16} \times 7\frac{13}{16}$ (27 × 19·8). Gift of Mrs. Donald B. Straus

buildings clashing with the sky with the minute and insignificant dwellers of such magnificent space.

Generally, the other artists who lived in Paris during the years when Cubism was developing did not make prints that reflected their alignment with the basic Cubist forms. Léger made his first print in 1920, well after his interest in machines had entirely changed his methods of composition. However, this historical survey is primarily interested in the classical print as it was transformed in modern times, and for this reason Léger's designs for Blaise Cendrars's *La Fin du Monde* (Editions de la Sirène, 1919) are important. The use of letter forms and color in a simultaneous yet fugal manner is, like the literary calligrammes of Apollinaire, a collage formula emerging out of Cubism. After the Cubists put letters (not always in the recognizable form of words) into their compositions, it was not surprising that letters themselves should become primary compositional elements. The plates from *La Fin du Monde* combine line block for the black areas and watercolor applied by brush through stencils. Stencil, at the moment when Léger needed it, was exclusively a commercial process. (*Pochoir*, the French word for stencil, implies the method of hand application used for Léger's illustrations.) Stencil was to be developed later into a more directly acknowledged fine-print medium, but the early date of Léger's illustrations negatively prejudiced attention toward them.

Before World War I Paris was the indisputable meeting ground for artists. There was great mobility among the fervent adherents to home-developed art movements, so that it was quite natural for Futurists from Italy to seek recognition and ideas in Paris, distill what they found, and move it on to England and back to Italy. Artists from Russia and Central Europe moved back and forth. Frank Kupka (who lived with the Duchamp brothers at Puteaux) and Marc Chagall (who lived in Paris from 1910 to 1914) partook of Delaunay's ideas. In the meantime, the Russian artists who remained home were able to view the marvelous collections of Sergei Shchukin and Ivan Morosov, which contained Cézannes and even Picasso's paintings done after 1907. The creation of the purist abstraction, De Stijl, in Holland was spurred by the return of Piet Mondrian from Paris during the war.

While there was considerable awareness of all the varieties of Cubist inspiration outside of Paris, there was little motivation to make prints

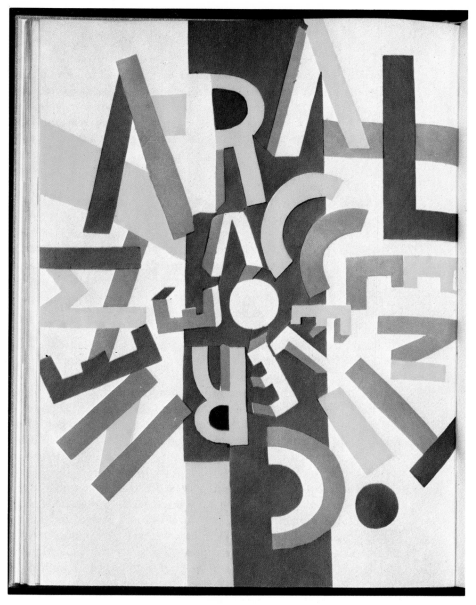

40 Fernand Léger:(1881–1955), page 41 from *La Fin du Monde* by Blaise Cendrars. Paris, La Sirène, 1919.
Pochoir, page 12½ × 9⅞ (31·7 × 25). Louis E. Stern Collection

on the part of those artists who were involved in the new esthetic. Lacking both the encouragement that Kahnweiler provided in Paris and the almost hereditary need that the Germans had to make prints, artists outside these two areas used their main energies to experiment and develop further paths toward abstraction. If artists in Paris had their difficulties coming to terms with the print media after the glorious 1890s, the artists of Italy existed in a printmaking void. Of the artists who were to participate in the most dynamic (and voluble) of the early twentieth-century art movements, Futurism, only Boccioni, Carrà, and Severini made prints. Boccioni's etchings precede his exposure to the force of the Parisian Cubists in 1911; Carrà's etchings were made after his involvement with de Chirico and Metaphysical painting; and Severini recapitulated and contemporized his Futurist imagery in color lithographs after World War II.

In England the Vorticist movement included two artists who made outstanding prints: Charles Wadsworth, whose woodcuts are the purest examples of Vorticist abstraction, and C. R. W. Nevinson, whose best wartime etchings parallel Boccioni's and Severini's paintings of that period.

An important concern became the creation of propaganda for the several abstract movements. Changed ideas about the relative values of elements in picture composition quite radically affected the typography of their various manifestoes. Such attention to public design by those deeply involved in personal painting became, after World War I, a significant part of the motivation behind the Bauhaus. The characteristic tendency toward the geometrical in abstract form nearly obliterated for a short time the more Expressionistic method of abstraction.

In Russia before the revolution of 1917, the inclination toward abstraction was considerable. In 1913 the publication in St. Petersburg of several pamphlets by the Russian Futurist poets gave Kasimir Malevich, Natalie Goncharova, and other artists the opportunity to create small lithographic illustrations. These are the few prints to show the Russian interpretation of Cubist and Futurist influences. Malevich's *Simultaneous Death of a Man in an Airplane and at the Railway* (1913) for the poem *Vzorval* (*Explodity*) by Alexei Kruchenyckh shows his assimilation of the contemporary iconology from which the Futurists derived their fresh and forceful imagery. Underlying the subject of simultaneity of experience in Malevich's

41

41 Kasimir Malevich (1878–1935), *Simultaneous Death of a Man in an Airplane and at the Railway* from *Vzorval* by Alexei Kruchenyckh. St. Petersburg, 1913. Lithograph, $3\frac{9}{16} \times 5\frac{1}{2}$ (9 × 14). Gift of Celeste Bartos

small lithograph is the structural strength of geometric form, which began to be distilled into the purity of Suprematism (a backdrop for Kruchenyckh's opera *Victory over the Sun* of 1913 was a black and white square). After the revolution, aiming toward cultural activity for all people, the Russian artists worked in all areas: theater, environment, propaganda. For a time, under Trotsky, ethnic revival was encouraged, and both Chagall and El Lissitzky worked on propagating a Jewish folk art through their painting and design. After Lenin's policies gained power, the artists became more restricted as to what activities they were allowed to participate in. As repression became suppression, they left Russia. They brought to their place of refuge, Germany for most, their well-established geometrical abstraction, which was to confront the adherents of Expressionism.

Chagall, as he passed through Berlin, executed his first prints, drypoints to illustrate his folk autobiography *My Life* (*Mein Leben*) (1922). The text was not published until many years later, but the prints, which are a combination of incidents with character portraits, tell the story well enough. Chagall's provincial fantasizing displays

42 Jacques Villon (Gaston Duchamp) (1875–1963), *Game of Solitaire*, 1903. Etching and aquatint, 13⅝ × 17⅝ (34·6 × 44). Abby Aldrich Rockefeller Fund

43 Erich Heckel (1883–1970), *Franzi Reclining*, 1910. Woodcut, 8 15/16 × 16 9/16 (22·7 × 42). Gift of Mr. and Mrs. Otto Gerson

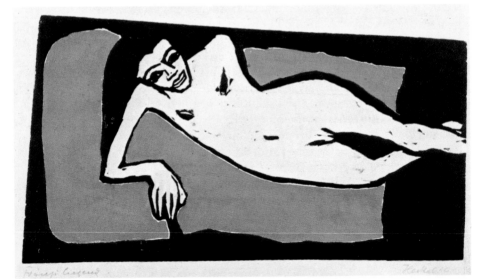

44 Georges Rouault (1871–1958), *Clown and Monkey*, 1910. Monotype, $22\frac{5}{8} \times 15\frac{1}{4}$ (57·5 × 38·7). Gift of Mrs. Sam A. Lewisohn

45 Emil Nolde (Emil Hansen) (1867–1956), *Young Couple*, 1913. Lithograph, $24\frac{7}{16} \times 20\frac{1}{16}$ (62 × 51). Purchase Fund

46 Marc Chagall (1889–1985), *The Grandfathers* from *Mein Leben*. Berlin, Paul
Cassirer, 1923. Drypoint, $10\frac{7}{8} \times 8\frac{1}{2}$ (27·6 × 21·6). A. Conger Goodyear Fund

occasionally vestigial Cubist influences. However, his dreamlike
visions are dependent upon a looser form of structure that developed
46 into a manner unique to Chagall. *The Grandfathers* from *My Life*
represents as well as any print of the 1920s the dilution of Cubism's
forms with narrative concerns.

4 Postwar Expressionism and nonobjective art in Germany

As we have seen, there was little diminution in the output of the German Expressionist artists after the war. Faced with disillusion, they had even more reason to pour out their feelings through their art. Younger artists, far more bitter in their approach, participated in the nihilistic Dada manifestations in Zürich and Cologne or contributed to a biting attack on mankind's weaknesses. The latter group of artists who evinced this 'new objectivity,' eager to rub the public nose in the moral decay of the times, made extensive use of graphic art. The most critical artists among them were George Grosz and Otto Dix. They represented in their prints not only the ugliness of the perpetrators of war but the vulgar decadence of those who wallowed

47 Otto Dix (1891–1969), *The War I, 6: Wounded (Fall 1916 Bepaume)*. Berlin, Nierendorf, 1924. Etching and aquatint, $7\frac{3}{4} \times 11\frac{3}{8}$ (19·6 × 28·9). Gift of Abby Aldrich Rockefeller

48 George Grosz (1893–1959), plate 5 from *Im Schatten*. Berlin, Malek, 1921. Lithograph, $14\frac{3}{4} \times 10\frac{5}{8}$ (37·5 × 27). Purchase

49 Ernst Ludwig Kirchner (1880–1938), *Winter Moonlight*, 1919. Woodcut, $12\frac{1}{16} \times 11\frac{5}{8}$ (30·6 × 29·5). Purchase Fund

in its aftermath. Grosz, in his portfolios *Im Schatten* and *Gott mit uns*,   *48* used his sharp wit to pinpoint the current immorality through the confrontation of broadly caricatured participants. Dix created in his portfolio of fifty etchings *War* (Berlin, Karl Nierendorf, 1924) a   *47* twentieth-century and decidedly Germanic counterpart to Francisco Goya's *Disasters of War* (1810–20). Dix illustrated with caustic candor the horrors of a battlefield peopled with half-human figures wearing the distinctive helmets of the German army.

Max Beckmann was a successful artist before the war. Returning from the medical corps and deeply moved by the discouraging state of German society, he was able, partly through a greater sensitivity to his media, to convey a more generalized view of this frenetic period than Dix and Grosz. His compositions often rely on the simultaneous representation of several facets of a subject and have much in them that recalls early Expressionism. His portfolio of large lithographs, *Die Hölle* (*Hell*) (1919), presents a panorama of the seamy life of the time under excruciatingly sharp magnification. The sprawling angular figures in *Night* (a painting of the same composition was made in 1918–19) from this portfolio are contained by a segmented background that gives the effect of seeing many aspects of life as through a prism. Beckmann often used this compositional system to offer more visual information than would ordinarily appear within a classical framework.

50

50 Max Beckmann (1884–1950), *Night* from *Die Hölle*, Berlin, J.B. Neumann, 1919. Lithograph, 21⅞ × 27⅝ (55·5 × 70). Purchase Fund

51 Max Beckmann (1884–1950),
Self Portrait with Bowler Hat, 1921.
Drypoint, $12\frac{5}{16} \times 9\frac{5}{8}$ ($31 \times 24\cdot4$).
Given anonymously

The simple portrait was turned into a container of considerable psychological complexity by the Expressionist artists of this time. Beckmann's *Self Portrait with Bowler Hat* (1921), in its first state, is a *51* contrived, theatrical presentation of the subject. The strong diagonals of studio paraphernalia are carried over into the world-weary expression of the artist's face. Even the bowler hat is formed from patches of angled lines made by the drypoint; the allover pattern of lines is used independent of the forms described. Oskar Kokoschka's tortured *Self Portrait* (1923) is far more brutal in its angularity. This Austrian *52* artist, who began to work in the Viennese Secession style, spent the early years of Expressionism illustrating his own poems and plays and representing subjects that lent themselves to extremely passionate execution. His highly charged gestural line in the many lithographs he made both in the early decades of this century and a half a century later, while ever at the service of a recognizable subject, was one of the links between the Expressionist movements of those two periods.

59

52 Oskar Kokoschka (1886–1980), *Self Portrait*, 1923. Lithograph, $24\frac{1}{2} \times 18\frac{3}{8}$ (62·2 × 46·6). Purchase Fund

53 Josef Albers (1888–1976), *Self Portrait*, 1917. Transfer lithograph, 18½ × 12 (47 × 30·5). John B. Turner Fund

An earlier portrait by an artist who was going to follow an entirely different path is Josef Albers's *Self Portrait* (1917). This crayon litho-   53
graph, in which the surface is broken up into facets, is a student's attempt to construct human form from geometric elements. Like much of the regional reaction to Cubism, only the superficial elements remain. However, Albers was to go on, first as a student and then as a master, at the Bauhaus, distilling the ideas he took from Cubism: fragmentation and simultaneity. Although in the years of his association with the Bauhaus he made few prints, his study of

light and color during his work in stained glass there played a major role in printmaking four decades later.

Lyonel Feininger, Wassily Kandinsky, and Paul Klee were earlier masters at the Bauhaus. The architect Walter Gropius took over the Weimar Schools of Arts and Crafts in 1919 and combined them into the unique institution of the State Bauhaus. There, throwing together artists, craftsmen, and architects, he insisted that all should have practical experience and that all minds should be open to the rising idea that there was a 'universal unity in which all opposing forces exist in a state of balance.'[8] In practice this led to the integration of the visual and practical arts by dividing the teaching of each subject into form and craft. Since the substructure of the Bauhaus was architectural, it was to be expected that geometrical elements became more pronounced in the work of some of the mature artists. Feininger's woodcuts, which he cut in sharp rectangular forms or straight lines, were most often of architectural views. If they pictured landscape alone, it was generally of the sea, and the strong horizon became a foundation for the prismatic rendering of the effect of light in the sky and on water. His woodcut for the cover of the Bauhaus manifesto of 1919 combines a concern for structure (a cathedral!) with the idealism of a new spiritual movement (Socialism).

Paul Klee joined the Bauhaus in 1920. He had experienced many influences before the war, including that of Der Blaue Reiter and the romantic atmosphere of Tunisia, but he was able to clarify his attitude toward the creation of art only at the Bauhaus. There he was motivated to convey to the students the processes from which creative acts emerged. At the same moment as he was compiling his thoughts, he was exposed to the strong geometrical abstract forces from Holland (van Doesburg taught in Weimar, though not at the Bauhaus) and from Russia (Kandinsky joined the Bauhaus in 1922 after having purged his work of natural motifs under the influence of the Suprematists and Constructivists). However, Klee rarely discarded the human or naturalist element from his compositions. His fantasizing upon the observations he continually made of nature and human nature found form quite frequently in an imaginative childlike rendering. He often allowed his etching style to freely find an image on the plate. He made use of a technique similar to frottage (rubbing) by drawing his forms over wet ink, which produced a blotted and grainy monotype. (Gauguin had created a series of monotypes by

54 Lyonel Feininger (1871–1956), *Cathedral*
(*Bauhaus program*), 1919. Woodcut, 12 × 7½
(30·4 × 19). Gift of Abby Aldrich Rockefeller

this method in the early 1900s.) In Klee's lithograph *Tightrope
Walker* (1923) the black lines are produced by this type of transfer.   55
For all the rhythmic, straight, intersecting lines and abstract color
planes, Klee's special sense of satire remains deftly balanced. During
that same year, 1923, Kandinsky was to create his finest lithograph   *56*
in the full geometric style that was to remain his until his death. He
had, the year before, produced a portfolio of etchings, woodcuts,
and lithographs (*Kleine Welten*, 1922) which are a visual survey of
his formal progress from Expressionist abstraction after nature to a
more rigid structuralization. Always more romantic than his Constructivist contemporaries, Kandinsky continued to insinuate variable
forms (such as the three double lumps on the right) which, with the
mathematically impure arrangement of his compositional elements,
promote a mystical interpretation.

56 Wassily Kandinsky (1866–1944), *Orange*, 1923. Lithograph, 16 × 15⅛ (40·6 × 38·4). Purchase Fund

55 (*left*) Paul Klee (1879–1940), *Tightrope Walker*, 1923. Transfer lithograph, 17⅛ × 10⅝ (43·5 × 27). Given anonymously

57 Lázló Moholy-Nagy (1895–1946), plate 1 from *Konstruktionen*, 1923. Hanover, Ludwig Ey, 1923. Lithograph, $23\frac{5}{8} \times 17\frac{15}{16}$ (60 × 45·5). Lent anonymously

58 El Lissitzky (Lazar Markovitch) (1890–1941), plate 1 from *Proun*. Hanover, Ludwig Ey, 1923. Lithograph, $14 \times 13\frac{9}{16}$ (35·5 × 34·4). Purchase Fund

In 1923 the Bauhaus held its first exhibition, and a new faculty member was introduced, the Hungarian Lázló Moholy-Nagy. Just two years before he had met El Lissitzky, the Russian Constructivist who, like Kandinsky, left his homeland for Germany in 1921. The 57 lithographs made by the Hungarian innovator in the arts of design, 58 light, and motion, and those made in the same year by Lissitzky, who was the catalytic figure in the merging of the Russian, Dutch, and German ideas of nonobjective art, reveal not only similarities but the tentative emergence of a new graphic medium. Mechanically produced tones, lines drawn with a ruler, the techniques and materials of the designer were used to create works of art made up of pure geometrical shapes. The Kestner-Gesellschaft in Hanover, set up in 1916, chose Lissitzky and Moholy-Nagy to create portfolios of prints for the organization's first publications of original works in 1923. These photomechanical prints, like those of Kurt Schwitters of the same year, occupied a strange no-man's-land in relation to fine printmaking of the time, but their fundamental place in the evolution of the twentieth-century print is now well established.

66

5   Dada and Surrealism

As WORLD WAR I gained momentum, a group of artists and writers promoted an irreverent view of all human endeavor in their demonstrations, writings, and exhibitions in Zürich. From these first manifestations at the Café Voltaire in 1916, which became known as Dada, arose the ideas that characterized the early work of Jean Arp, an Alsatian writer and artist in exile in Switzerland, and Max Ernst, a participant with Arp in the postwar Dadaist activities in Cologne. Basic to all forms of Dada-inspired work was anti-logic. Rather than use established forms of art for criticism or reflection, as the artists of the Neue Sachlichkeit did, the Dadaists wished to disencumber themselves of all tradition, since even the known structures of art were part of the virulent structure of society. Dada was a point of view, not a movement, and as such was vitally international. In New York Duchamp put the concept of a 'work of art' to test with his ready-mades. Francis Picabia had forecast as early as 1912 the nonsense vein of Dada by the titles he invented for his paintings. He was also in New York during World War I and promoted the anarchistic and witty spirit that was a sort of Dada in Alfred Stieglitz's publications *Camera Work* and *291*. He joined the Zürich group in 1916 and later played a part in the Paris demonstrations. Although neither artist created prints in editions during this period, their personal contributions at the time of Dada to the roadways that were to be followed decades later will be seen to have been extremely significant.

As the Dada nihilism and irreverence spread, those who participated began to create permanent objects (Richard Huelsenbeck, one of the poets in the group and the probable originator of the term 'Dada,' published *Die Phantastische Gebete* illustrated by Arp in 1916) and promote exhibitions of examples of art they felt were revolutionary (Kandinsky, Kokoschka, Marc, and Picasso). Huelsenbeck returned to

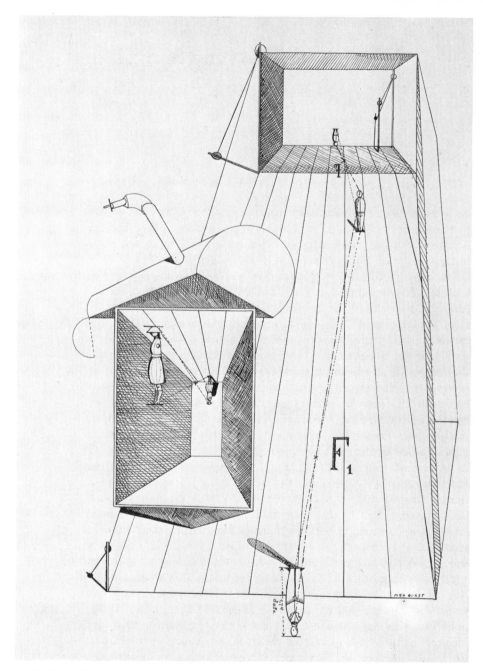

59 Max Ernst (1891–1976), plate from *Fiat Modes, Pereat Ars.* Cologne, Schlömilch, 1919. Lithograph, $15\frac{3}{4} \times 10\frac{3}{8}$ (40 × 26·3). Purchase Fund

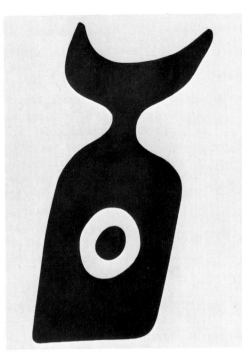

60 Jean (Hans) Arp (1887–1966), *Navel Bottle*
from *Arpaden*. Hanover, Merz, 1923.
Lithograph, 16⅜ × 9¾ (41·6 × 24·7). Gift of
J. B. Neumann

Berlin in 1917 and, with Grosz and Raoul Hausmann, among others, promoted the most important Dada exhibition in 1920. That year he wrote, 'Dada was to give the truth a new impetus. Dada was to be a rallying point for abstract energies and a lasting slingshot for the great international artistic movements.'[9]

After the war Max Ernst returned from the battlefields to Cologne. He was aware of Zürich Dada through his friend Arp, and was also drawn to the work of Alfred Kubin, Paul Klee, and Giorgio de Chirico. His first prints under these influences were contained in an album *Let There Be Fashion, Down with Art (Fiat Modes, Pereat Ars)* 59 (1919). Drafted with the care of a mechanical drawing incorporating the expected elements of perspective sightings and measurements, this transfer lithograph from the album juxtaposes the anticipated with the impossible. As the title definitively explains, tradition is not to be venerated, up is down, in is out.

In 1915–16 Arp was creating automatic drawings, that is, allowing chance to define form. Although Klee had used a similar technique to discover later a subject within the unguided lines he set upon paper,

Arp's lines tended to create abstract compositions of ambiguous natural forms. For Arp this combination of chance with the irrational amalgamation of life forms (which appeared in his poetry as well as his visual art) eventually found form in the portfolio of prints known as *Arpaden* (1923). The single images are totally imaginary, and *Navel* *Bottle* is the most elaborate conjunction of the familiar placed outside nature. The stark contrast of black and white lifts the image away from the paper in the manner of Arp's jig-sawed wood reliefs of the time.

60

Arpaden was a Merz publication, the review issued by the German Dadaist Kurt Schwitters, who promoted his idea of using cast-off materials to create his world view[10] under the catchall title 'Merz' (from 'Kommerz,' a word in an advertisement used in one of his collages). Working in Hanover, where Lissitzky had settled, Schwitters published his *Merz* review from 1923 until 1932. Schwitters's Merz portfolio of his own prints was a photomechanical collage; like those of Lissitzky of the same year, a few examples had added collage elements. Schwitters oddly juxtaposed familiar images, but also introduced a structure of geometric forms and obliterated expected details by manipulating the transcription of the individual elements. Many of the prints incorporate lettering, the natural visual detritus of Schwitters's contemporary culture.

61

The early years of the 1920s saw the migration of the Zürich Dadaists in several directions. Tristan Tzara, the spokesman, found his way to Paris in 1920, and with other young writers (Aragon, Breton, and Eluard) he participated in the earliest Parisian Dadaist manifestations. By 1922 a struggle for philosophical primacy between Tzara and Breton heralded the end of the Dada period. Breton began his development of a specific Surrealist doctrine which culminated in a manifesto issued in 1924. His definition included 'pure psychic automatism' and 'the future resolution of the states of dream and reality . . . into a sort of absolute reality, or *surréalité*. . . .'[11] Taking Freud and certain areas of scientific thought as part of his foundation, Breton also revived interest in the Symbolist writers – those artists who made manifest in their poetry the very psychological aberrations from which Freud drew his theories.

Among the artists who concerned themselves with Breton's authoritarian movement were the former Dada artists Arp and Ernst; two young artists who had been involved with Cubism, André Masson and Joan Miró; a self-taught painter, Yves Tanguy; and the

Belgian René Magritte. It was not until the second period of Surrealism, after Breton's manifesto of 1929, that important prints
by any of the artists, other than book illustrations, were issued. The
Surreal object began to dominate automatic abstraction, and artists
such as Salvador Dali and Alberto Giacometti joined the movement.
During the 1930s the elements within the stylistic code of Surrealism
began to coalesce. The movement, which essentially was synonymous
with the close group surrounding Breton, continued to have a vital
influence into the 1940s, although it was spasmodically ruptured by
philosophical disagreements.

During the early, mainly theoretical, period of Surrealism the field
of fine prints lay outside Surrealist philosophy. A typical endeavor
that turned aside from the established formulae for art forms was
Max Ernst's album *Histoire Naturelle* (1926). This was a collection of
collotypes of frottages, the technique of rubbing that Ernst developed
as a method of removing his conscious self from the making of
images. *Une Semaine de Bonté ou Les Sept éléments capitaux* (five   63
volumes, Paris, Jeanne Bucher, 1934) was a series of reproductions
of collages made from wood-engravings of the late nineteenth
century. The personal juxtaposition of persons, animals, and objects
immediately conveys a sense of the frightening aspects of memory

61 Kurt Schwitters (1887–1948), plate 4
from *Merz* portfolio. Hanover, Merz,
1923. Photo-lithograph, $21\frac{7}{8} \times 17\frac{1}{4}$
(53.6×43.8). Gift of J. B. Neumann

62 Joan Miró (1893–1983), *Equinox*, 1968. Etching and aquatint, $41\frac{1}{16} \times 29$ (104.3 × 73.7). Gift of Studebaker-Worthington, Inc.

63 Max Ernst (1891–1976), plate 25 from *Une Semaine de Bonté*, vol. 4. Paris, J. Bucher, 1934. Line block, $10\frac{7}{8} \times 8\frac{5}{8}$ (27·6 × 22). Louis E. Stern Collection

and dream. Ernst described his concept of collage in 1936: 'A ready-made reality, whose naïve destination has the air of having been fixed, once and for all (a canoe), finding itself in the presence of another and hardly less absurd reality (a vacuum cleaner), in a place where both of them must feel displaced (a forest), will, by this very fact, escape to its naïve destination and to its identity; it will pass from its false absolute, through a series of relative values, into a new absolute value, true and poetic: canoe and vacuum cleaner will make love. The mechanism of collage, it seems to me, is revealed by this very simple example . . . the coupling of two realities, irreconcilable in appearance, upon a plane which apparently does not suit them.'[12] The 175 collages in the five volumes are not interrupted by text and so form an extended visual experience considerably broader and more detailed than a single picture. By using visual material from a time in the past, Ernst seems to have introduced in this and several preceding

64 André Masson (1896–1987), plate 2 from *Soleils Bas* by Georges Limbour. Paris, Galerie Simon, 1924. Drypoint, page $9\frac{1}{2} \times 7\frac{5}{8}$ (24 × 19·3). Gift of Walter P. Chrysler, Jr.

65 (*right*) André Masson (1896–1987), *Rape*, 1941. Drypoint, $12\frac{1}{8} \times 16$ (30·8 × 40·6). Lent anonymously

books the element of nostalgia that pervaded much Surrealist imagery. Works created in the 1960s, particularly by Eduardo Paolozzi and R. B. Kitaj, utilized collage in the same disjointed narrative form that Ernst created in *Une Semaine de Bonté*. While Ernst was to go on to create prints in the established and traditional media, his early use of the printed image was innovative.

Like the first Cubist prints, the earliest examples of the so-called 'fine-print' media that presented Surrealist imagery appeared as illustrations in books published by Daniel-Henry Kahnweiler. The young André Masson had been a casualty of World War I, and after his confinement in a psychiatric hospital he spent several years exploring modern painting, from Impressionism to Cubism. In 1922 he became a member of Kahnweiler's Galerie Simon, and before his first exhibition there in 1923 he became acquainted with Breton and joined the group that was to become the Surrealists. His first prints were drypoints illustrating Georges Limbour's *Soleils Bas* (Galerie Simon, 1924), and as they date from the year of the first Surrealist

64

manifesto, they could be considered the first Surrealist prints.[13] However, their formal structure is still too well defined to allow them to accurately reflect Breton's credo, 'pure psychic automatism, by which one intends to express . . . the real functioning of the mind.'[14] Subsequent illustrations for Robert Desnos's *C'est les bottes des sept lieues cette phrase: 'Je me vois'* (Galerie Simon, 1926) show that Masson was able to break his dependence upon Cubistic structure and give free rein to the intricate imagery of his subconscious.

Masson's adherence to Surrealist tenets was broken in 1933. However, he returned to Breton's fold in 1937 and the next year contributed an etching to Paul Eluard's small portfolio *Solidarité*. Like many of the artists and writers who fled to the U.S.A. during World War II, he used the rare moment of camaraderie among the Surrealists to begin a thorough exploration of automatism and sub-consciously derived imagery. *Rape* (1941), created in Masson's studio in Connecticut, is one of the few totally automatic prints. Although it was not printed until 1957, it is the purest expression of the Surrealist

65

philosophy that was to inspire American artists, unencumbered by contrived subject-matter. He became a prolific maker of prints in New York, where Curt Valentin played Kahnweiler's role in the promotion of editions and illustrated books. Again, in 1943, Masson broke with Breton, and subsequent works began to show elements derived from a confrontation with reality rather than released from the subconscious. The strong calligraphic tendency arising from automatism becomes a linear network in the etching *Chinese Actors* (1957), while color quite often has the scintillating appearance of pure Impressionism, particularly in the forty lithographs for his reminiscence, *Voyage à Venise* (1952).

It was Masson who introduced his neighbor Joan Miró to André Breton in 1924. Lacking the connection with Kahnweiler, Miró did not produce any prints during the early years of Surrealism. His first prints were small lithographs for Tristan Tzara's *L'Arbre des Voyageurs* (Paris, Montaigne, 1930). Three years later, he produced three etchings for Georges Hugnet's *Enfances* (Paris, Cahiers d'Art, 1933). These plates show biomorphic shapes in opposition to rigid horizontal lines. The appearance of soft, rather unstructured forms and indications of a distant horizon lend a sense of the timeless and placeless that seems related only to the subconscious. Indeed, as late as 1948 Miró insisted that his subconscious gave the initial impetus to a composition, but it was equally important to discipline these impulses and give them final structure.[15] Miró had associated with the writers of the Surrealist movement from their Dadaist period, and Breton described him as 'the most surrealist of us all.'[16] His work epitomized the visual possibilities of the Surrealist doctrine even though he did not go through the excessively exotic behavior that characterized Dali's concept of a totally Surrealist life. Miró was not a card-carrying Surrealist, and it was his independence from Breton's overwhelming dogmatism that allowed him to work so freely with his chosen imagery. After his tenuous book illustrations of the early 1930s, Miró was to develop into a major printmaker. His brief association with Louis Marcoussis, who had set up a print workshop in 1933, resulted in a number of vigorous drypoints including a series in red and black and a *Self Portrait* (1938), on which Marcoussis also worked.

The Spanish Civil War had its effect upon the Spanish-born artists living in France, and Miró's art developed a fierce, angry character, which he modulated during his return to Spain during World War II.

66 Joan Miró (1893–1983), plate 1 from *Enfances* by Georges Hugnet. Paris, Cahiers d'art, 1933. Etching, page 11 × 8¾ (28 × 22). Louis E. Stern Collection.

67 Joan Miró (1893–1983), *Barcelona Series XXIII*, 1944. Lithograph, 24⅜ × 18 9/16 (62 × 47). Purchase Fund

His transfer lithographs known as the *Barcelona Series* (drawn in 1939   67
but not printed until 1944) show the manner in which his inherent
sense of the wry has been modified by the presence of elements
denoting threat or impending danger. The Barcelona prints, fifty
compositions in all, brought Miró face to face with the immense
creative possibilities in printmaking. In 1947 he went to the U.S.A.,
where he was to execute a mural for the Terrace Hilton Hotel in
Cincinnati, Ohio. In New York, where he painted the mural, he
found Stanley William Hayter's displaced Atelier 17. In that workshop Miró learned many new intaglio techniques as well as old ones,
such as the relief etching method pioneered by the nineteenth-century
mystic artist and poet William Blake. Miró used this latter method for
a few prints issued in America and for several series published by his
dealer Aimé Maeght in 1952–53. *Series I*, also known as *The Family*,   68
in its eight variations of inking, is one of Miró's most successful
prints. The composition is enhanced by the colors, which are used in
an entirely new manner. Miró's work in ceramics during this period

seems to have influenced to some extent the complete separation of the figures and the incised nature of their outlines and interior details. His imagery returns to a more joyful tone; the signs of stars, birds, suns, and physical parts so peculiar to Miró combine in harmonious accord.

Miró's pictographic style utilized a well-developed but functionally limited symbology which allowed for a certain breadth of interpretation but also had the elements of exact meaning. The symbols were constantly at the mercy of compositional requirements and became transmogrified by variations in Miró's calligraphic rendering. He found an affinity with the Oriental letter symbols, which were so *62* dependent on agile brushwork. In the monumental *Equinox* (1968) executed in his seventy-fifth year, Miró devised signs for the changing seasons and made of them a huge cipher containing within it the intimation of a human or godlike presence. Surrounded by stars and

68 Joan Miró (1893–1983), *Series I*, plate IV (*The Family*), 1952. Etching and engraving $14\frac{15}{16} \times 17\frac{7}{8}$ (38 × 45.4). Curt Valentin Bequest

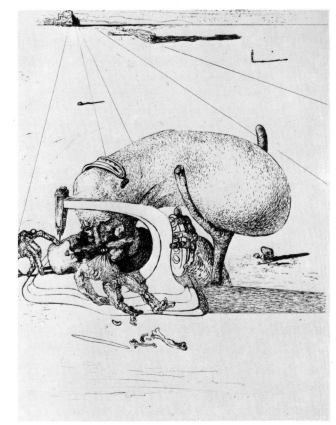

69 Salvador Dali (b. 1904), plate XIV from *Les Chants de Maldoror* by Comte de Lautréamont. Paris, Skira, 1934. Etching, page $13\frac{1}{8} \times 10\frac{1}{8}$ (33.3×25.7). Louis E. Stern Collection

suns, this monolithic form holds the terrific force of the unknown. While there is a pleasurable character to Miró's work in general, most of it includes a degree of mystery that seems related not only to Surrealism but also to the unique personality of the Spanish.

The art of the Surrealists began to find acceptance in the 1930s and consequently more luxurious and less experimental works were put into production. A book by one of the father-figures of the movement, Isadore Ducasse, known as Comte de Lautréamont, was illustrated by Salvador Dali. The forty-two etchings for *Les Chants de Maldoror* (Paris, Albert Skira, 1934), while not Dali's first, do epitomize the Surrealist concepts as they found visual form. For Dali, drawing and etching were almost identical tasks. He saw nothing unique in the print media and so did not exploit their potential. He created his work through 'paranoic-critical activity,' which he

69

described as a 'spontaneous method of *"irrational knowledge,"* based on the critical and systematic objectification of delirious associations and interpretations.' [17] Most of the etchings include familiar Daliesque motifs: distant perspectives, soft shapes held by crutches, bones, long shadows, and so on. He wrote in *Conquest of the Irrational* (New York, Julien Levy, 1935), '. . . be persuaded that Salvador Dali's famous limp watches are nothing else than the tender, extravagant and solitary paranoic-critical camembert of time and space,' which James Thrall Soby interpreted as 'a clue to one of the painter's most fervid obsessions – his pre-occupation with malleability . . . which leads him to convert hard objects, like watches, into substances soft as camembert.' [18] One plate shows a hydrocephalic head, supported by a crutch, biting into a woman's breast while her head is held under the needle of a sewing machine. Draped over the soft head is a soft watch indicating twelve o'clock, while lines of perspective shoot off into a mysterious landscape populated by skulls, bones, and figures casting long shadows.

Dali was cast out of the Surrealist circle several times for various reasons, such as his interest in Nazism and his tendency towards conscious self-glorification. It is certain that during the 1940s he proceeded to paint on a monumental scale and produce works that attracted rather than alienated a wider public. His prints, too, appealed to that part of the population that found the strange conjunction of images and well-known subjects (*Don Quixote, Alice in Wonderland,* to name only two of the suites published in the 1960s) titillating and as imaginative as a Hollywood Technicolor dream. While few of his prints of mid-century are much more than reproductions of drawings and watercolors, Dali, for all his romanticism and narcissism, created a unique visual language which he has continued to brandish in provocative ways (as in his hologram of 1973).

An event in the history of twentieth-century printmaking that was to have repercussions in the future of painting was the entry of the British geologist Stanley William Hayter into the field of art. After a short scientific career, he set up a studio in Paris and became acquainted with several members of the Surrealist group, with whom he exhibited in 1933. In that year he moved to 17 rue Campagne-Première, where his print workshop first acquired its name, Atelier 17. He had been experimenting with the various intaglio techniques (drypoint, engraving, etching, and so forth) since 1926. His innovations in the medium drew many artists to his studio, where they too found the many new possibilities of intaglio both intriguing and inspiring. Hayter's method was based on the theory of automatism: he would allow his graver (burin) to cut freely into the plate, propelled only by the undirected movements of his one hand while his other, also undirected, moved the plate around. Upon the unconscious linear pattern thus obtained, Hayter added areas of tone, reinforced and elaborated upon the lines, and created from these mechanical workings his compositions, which generally incorporated one or more human figures as their subject.

Automatism was not considered an important concern during the second period of Surrealism (after 1929), but through Hayter's particular usage it became one of the last remnants of Surrealist influence when he set up his Atelier in New York during World War II. In New York he created *Amazon* (1945), which illustrates several 70 of the complex technical devices he used. The sweeping original automatic lines are still apparent as the basic structure of the composition, which is overlaid with soft-ground etching made from different fabrics. The lines have been deepened in places and occasionally cut so deeply that, printed without ink, they remain in white relief.

Hayter's influence upon American art during and shortly after the war will be discussed later. During the early years of his career as doyen of a print workshop, however, he did encourage some of his friends to make prints. The earliest prints of the sculptor Alberto Giacometti, Hayter's first neighbor in Paris, were made at Atelier 17 shortly after Hayter moved there. Between 1929 and 1935 Giacometti was a formal participant in the Surrealist movement, and generally his sculptures consisted of disturbing spatial constructions that arose from imagination or dream rather than reality. He developed a cagelike structure that contained and restrained disconcerting objects. Conveyed in these works was a sense of both mystery and frustration. At the time that he sculpted the rigidly frontalized *Invisible Object (Hands Holding the Void)* (1934–35), which was 71 simultaneously the subject of one of his first prints, Giacometti was turning away from the Surrealist's dependence upon the subconscious derivation of subject and form and returning to the exploration of nature. The frame-throne and the board that confines the legs (perhaps a reference to a prie-dieu) act as less of a mysterious enclosure, and the recognizably female form itself presents the human dilemma.

Giacometti never delved into the diverse processes of printmaking to any degree, although he created many prints in his lifetime. Most of his etchings and lithographs were part of the agonizing struggle to discover an inner truth in human form that occupied him between 1945 and his death in 1966.

Giorgio de Chirico, whose Metaphysical paintings of the period during World War I formed a historic steppingstone for the Surrealists, was rejected by Breton and other Surrealists in 1928. All his prints appeared after this moment and lack the qualities for which his work was admired during the 1920s. However, one artist whose artistic career was ignited by his admiration for de Chirico was Yves Tanguy. Self-taught, he gravitated toward the Surrealists, who recognized him officially in 1926. It was during the 1930s that he invented for his paintings a rather limited vocabulary, to which he persistently clung until his death in 1955. The etching of about 1938, *The Island of a Day*, is one of his few prints. The cumulative bone and ribbon formation against an unconfirmed and mysterious space creates a disturbingly unstable sense. Basic to Tanguy's imagery is the possibility that the object is real rather than transformed, so the viewer

70 Stanley William Hayter (b. 1901), *Amazon*, 1945. Engraving and etching, 24½ × 15⅞ (62·2 × 40·3). Philip C. Johnson Fund

71 Alberto Giacometti (1901–1966), *Hands Holding the Void*, 1934–35. Engraving, 12 × 9⅜ (30·4 × 24·5). Gift of Victor S. Riesenfeld

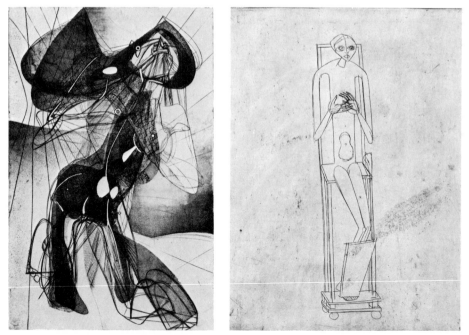

strives to discover its true identity. He illustrated three books during the 1930s, thus fulfilling what seems to have been a duty on the part of Surrealist artists to collaborate with Surrealist authors. He was one of the few exiled artists to remain in the U.S.A. after World War II and continue work in the Surrealist idiom.

The final period of direct esthetic influence of the members of the original Surrealist group occurred during World War II in New York. The youngest Surrealist was Matta, who had studied architecture before leaving his native Chile for Paris. His commitment to painting took place only two years before he fled to New York in 1939. In the U.S.A. his personal style moved away from the early inspiration of Tanguy as he developed a species of humanoids and spinning planes that replaced relatively impersonal forms. He made his first prints in New York, contributing an etching to Breton's book *Arcane 17* (New York, Brentano's, 1944) and participating with Ernst, Masson, Tanguy, and others in the *Brunidor Portfolio* (1947), a group of etchings and lithographs with an introduction by Nicolas Calas. Of Matta's print, *I Want to See It to Believe It*, Calas wrote, 'It is the story-portrait of the narcissist wounded in his pride, of the

72 Yves Tanguy (1900–1955), *The Island of a Day*, c. 1938. Etching, 7¾ × 3¹¹⁄₁₆ (19·7 × 9·4). Given anonymously

73 Matta (Sebastian Antonio Matta Echaurren) (b. 1912), *I Want to See It to Believe It* from *Brunidor Portfolio No. I*. New York, Brunidor, 1947. Lithograph, 12⅛ × 12⅞ (30·8 × 32·7). Purchase

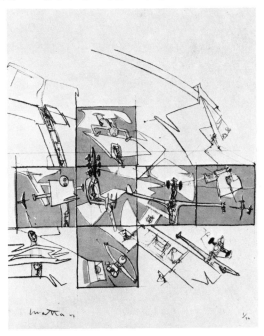

dandy admiring his wound; it is the drama of isolation portrayed on a cross, now situated in the stratosphere.'[19]

Matta became a more than occasional printmaker, and his personal method of making soft-ground color etchings resulted in some of the most vibrant Surrealist prints. One of his best friends in New York had been the American painter and critic Robert Motherwell, who was to become one of the vital links between the older movement and the incipient New York school of Abstract Expressionism. Another late Surrealist, the Swiss painter and printmaker Kurt Seligmann, taught Motherwell engraving. Seligmann made several albums of engravings and with the Cuban Wifredo Lam, who was probably the last to join the Paris group before it was driven away by the war, contributed to the *Brunidor Portfolio* devoted to the Surrealists.

After the war, when most of these artists returned to Paris, they continued on their individual ways, illustrating books and eventually participating in the print boom of the 1960s. Activity in the field of printmaking became so potent that even those few Surrealists who had never attempted work in the print media were induced to create editions. Among the débutants was Hans Bellmer, who made his first prints at the end of the war (1944) and re-created his erotic girl-puppets in sensitive engravings made by his own hand, most often after his drawings. Later René Magritte and Paul Delvaux, the Belgian Surrealists, made their first prints, but Magritte died before creating more than etched souvenirs, and Delvaux sought to find his special equilibrium in lithography only after his seventieth year.

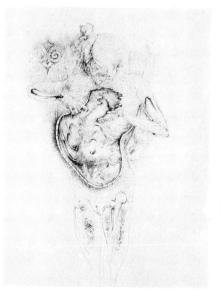

74

74 Hans Bellmer (1902–1975), *Rose ou verte la nuit*, 1966. Etching, $11\frac{3}{4} \times 7\frac{7}{8}$ (29·8 × 20). Mrs. Alfred R. Stern Fund

6 Independent directions: the School of Paris and the revival of lithography

WHILE TRACING THE BIRTH and growth of the major European movements it has been impossible to introduce the simultaneous evolution of those artists who grew beyond their early stylistic allegiances into unique and not neatly classifiable personalities. Foremost among them were Rouault, Matisse, Braque, and Picasso. In France there were, in addition, many other gifted painters who made prints and belonged to no specific school. Throughout Europe during the decades between the two World Wars many fine prints took forms that were traditional studio subjects or otherwise removed from the mainstreams of communal artistic purpose.

Almost exclusively concerned with religious or moral themes, Georges Rouault began his serious work as a maker of prints in 1916. His paintings and gouaches were executed in a stained-glass style that he had learned as a youth while studying the restoration of windows. Broad black lines, like leading, enclosed heavily shaded and colored forms. Since 1913 Ambroise Vollard had admired his paintings, and in 1916 he commissioned Rouault to create for him several series of prints. Rouault's ink drawings and paintings made for this purpose were photoengraved onto copper plates. He would then rework these mechanically made plates with a multitude of classic and unusual tools, and add freely drawn plates (usually in aquatint) which provided the dramatic heavy black outlines for the composition. In the mid-1930s the printer Roger Lacourière showed Rouault how color could be added to his prints by means of aquatint, and many of his earlier black and white subjects were revised and made into color prints. Rouault's foremost printed work was the great series of fifty-eight etchings, *Miserere* (commissioned by Vollard but published by L'Etoile Filante [Rouault] in 1948). These fifty-eight plates were part of what was proposed to be a larger two-volume work titled

75 Georges Rouault (1871–1958), *Who does not paint a face for himself?*, plate 8 from *Miserere*, 1922; published 1948. Etching, aquatint and heliogravure, $22\frac{5}{16} \times 16\frac{15}{16}$ (56·7 × 43). Gift of the artist

76 (*right*) Georges Rouault (1871–1958), *Autumn*, 1933. Lithograph, $17\frac{1}{2} \times 23$ (44·5 × 58·4). Gift of the artist

Miserere et Guerre. The plates that were ultimately published concern both mercy and war, of course, and are a highly dramatic portrayal of Christian subjects juxtaposed with satirical and scathingly bitter representations of human nature.

While the series contains several representations of the Crucifixion, death in various guises, devastated landscapes, and mocking portraits of the once-powerful, the themes are brought together in the resigned expression of a clown: 'Who does not paint a face for himself?'
75 (*Miserere*, plate 8, *c.* 1922, published in 1948). From the time of his monotype in 1910 Rouault's bittersweet attitude toward life could be best summed up in the personage of a clown. Rouault alluded to himself as a clown in his self portraits and it has often been assumed that this plate from *Miserere* is also a portrait of the artist.

Although Rouault produced a quantity of lithographs, mostly published in the late 1920s by E. Frapier's Galerie des Peintres-Graveurs (*Souvenirs Intimes, Démagogie, Cirque Forain*) and Editions des Quatre Chemins (*Petite Banlieue*), his most famous works were those undertaken for Vollard. The large black and white lithograph
76 *Autumn* (1933) was the major work in this medium. More popular, however, have been the color aquatints that appeared in the several illustrated books Rouault labored over for years. To most they best evoke the mood of Rouault's paintings. However, he did not work on the color plates themselves. They are, in the longer tradition of fine

printmaking, the result of the incredible skill of a master craftsman, Roger Lacourière. After Rouault drew the black plates (usually sugar-lift aquatint), Lacourière would make the color plates with the same subtlety as he obtained in reproducing a watercolor. In this manner were produced two large plates, *Christ on the Cross* and *Autumn*, illustrations for *Cirque de l'Etoile Filante* (Paris, Vollard, *83* 1938) and André Suares's *Passion* (Paris, Vollard, 1939), as well as the suites of color prints, *Cirque* and *Les Fleurs du Mal* (1938).

Henri Matisse followed his Fauve prints of 1906 with some exquisitely pure, linear lithographs, etchings, and monotypes of nudes, portraits, and still lifes in 1914. His sure and sensitive line distinguishes the best of his printed works, but his artistry as a painter and sculptor occasionally led to quite elaborate lithographic compositions wherein modeling and considerable detail add the dimension to which line only alludes. Perhaps the most imposing print of this sort is the large lithograph *Odalisque in Striped Pantaloons* (1925). This is the last in a *77* set of three compositions based on a model seated in a draped armchair. A fireplace in the background has been eliminated in this version, and the chair with its floral pattern is nearly *en face*, in opposition to the oblique pose of the model. The clashing patterns of the pantaloons and chair cover are mediated by the softly shaded contours of the flesh. All Matisse's lithographs were executed with crayon, either on transfer paper or directly upon the stone. Because the art of drawing from the model was so basic to his creative life, it appears that Matisse saw printmaking as only another outlet for his need to express himself by this means.

Because of his sublime sense of the value and optic weight of line, Matisse was able to create one of the most beautiful illustrated books of the first half of this century. The delicate balance between text and illustration is nowhere better achieved than in the volume of Stéphane Mallarmé's *Poésies* (Lausanne, Albert Skira, 1932). Matisse wrote, 'The problem was to balance each pair of facing pages – the one with the etching white, the other with the typography relatively black. I achieved this by modifying my arabesques in such a way that the spectator's attention would be interested as much by the entire page as by the promise of reading the text.'[20] The uniformly thin, etched lines fall upon the page in rhythmic patterns in a sort of extended echo of the cadence of the type forms and the inner meter of the poems themselves. The use of plates larger than the sheet size of the book allows the etched lines complete freedom of the page. This disrespect for margins dates back to Matisse's earliest lithographs and confirms his attitude toward printmaking as an extension of drawing.

78

77 Henri Matisse (1869–1954), *Odalisque in Striped Pantaloons*, 1925. Lithograph, $21\frac{1}{2} \times 17\frac{3}{8}$ (54·6 × 44). Nelson A. Rockefeller Bequest

78 Henri Matisse (1869–1954), plate 24 from *Poésies* by Stéphane Mallarmé. Lausanne, Skira, 1932. Etching, page 13 × 9¾ (33 × 24·7). Louis E. Stern Collection

Matisse returned to relief printmaking in the late 1930s with his linoleum-cut illustrations to Henry de Montherlant's *Pasiphaé – Chant de Minos (Les Crétois)* (Paris, Martin Fabiani, 1944). In these, as in his monotypes of 1914, the subjects are depicted in white line against black. Except for the dramatic shock of large black plates with thinly gouged lines, Matisse's approach to this medium is identical with his treatment of intaglio.

It was not until he became a partial invalid in 1941 that he produced a fresh approach to the printed image, and again this occurred not in the print workshop but in his studio, where it was an offshoot of his primary artistic endeavor. Matisse's use of cut and collaged colored paper began with the designs he made in 1931 for the three bays of Dr. Albert C. Barnes's art gallery in Merion, Pennsylvania. Several years later he executed a cover in this manner for *Verve* (Summer 1940), whose publisher, Efstratios Tériade, found the brilliance and ebullience of the colored paper collage extremely enchanting. During World War II he asked Matisse for more of these collages for an album in which Matisse was to write some of his thoughts. Although the illustrations for *Jazz* (Paris, Tériade, 1947), like many prints before and since, have been considered reproductions, they were printed under the artist's supervision by the stencil method, with the same paints Matisse had used to color the paper for the maquette collages. The method, however, is less important in this case than the result. The *Jazz* plates were the most brightly hued prints executed up to that time – the hard edges of each form abutting each other in an astonishing clash of colors. The prototype cover for *Verve*, which was created from cut-out printer's ink samples, appears pale and ephemeral compared with the fully saturated paint-box colors of *Jazz*. Most of the compositions have decorative borders, and each figure is given a generalized form that further emphasizes the positive nature of the two-dimensional space. *Horse, Rider and Clown* perfectly embodies Matisse's description of *Jazz*, 'The images in vivid and violent tones have resulted from crystallizations of memories of the circus, popular tales, or of travel.'[21]

86

Matisse found the formula by which he was able to translate the cut-outs of his studio into prints with all the desired properties: stunning and dense color, sharply defined shapes. The stencil process (*pochoir* in French, usually utilizing a brush rather than a spraygun or roller) which, until this time, was almost exclusively used for commercial art, became one of the favorite printing processes of the artists of the late 1960s in its more sophisticated form, silkscreen (serigraphy or screen printing).

Georges Braque, who was in the army during World War I, never resumed his close association with Picasso and their common Cubist explorations. Like Picasso he was eventually to find inspiration in ancient classical forms. In the early 1930s he evolved from the stylizations of Greek vase painting a linear style of figuration which he used in incised plaster and etchings. The subject of his suite of etchings of 1932, another of Vollard's unfinished projects, was Hesiod's *Theogony*. It was not issued as a book with text until 1955, but sixteen of the plates were printed in the 1930s. Meandering lines detail the archaic-appearing figures of the gods and the symbolic borders. There remains from his Cubist experience a tendency toward obscuring spatial definition that might create an illusion of depth, although the confining border is introduced as a boxlike container and becomes increasingly important as a compositional element in his later work.

79

When the *Theogony* plates finally were about to be printed in book form, two plates were found to be missing, so Braque had, in his late

79 Georges Braque (1882–1963), plate 3 from Hesiod: *Theogony*, 1932. Etching, $14\frac{3}{8} \times 11\frac{3}{4}$ ($36 \cdot 5 \times 29 \cdot 8$). Purchase Fund

sixties, to return to this subject of twenty years earlier. This led to further works on Greek mythological themes. Foremost among them was the depiction of the Helios myth. The first prints representing this subject were executed in 1946–48, and transcribe almost line for line a color lithograph of Athena and her chariot that Braque had made in 1932. The most dramatic versions of the Helios myth, however, are the prints titled *Chariot*, the first of which was printed in 1945 and is also titled *Phaedon*. In these lithographs the son of Helios is pulled in his father's chariot across the sky. The literal scene is set within a dark border which, in the last version (*The Varnished Chariot*, or *Chariot III*), becomes a highly varnished, lithographic shadow box.   *87*

These prints and the many still lifes as well as flower and bird illustrations for Braque's books were part of the significant revival of lithography that took place in Paris after World War II. There was a tendency in the late 1930s to introduce more color into prints, and through the learned encouragement of Roger Lacourière, both Rouault and

Picasso created brightly colored aquatints. However, during the period between the early years of the twentieth century and the end of World War II Paris saw very little in the area of color printmaking. The old workshops, where the colorful lithographs of the 1890s were created, had closed or were unable to stimulate interest among the great twentieth-century painters. The commercial lithography shop of Mourlot Frères concentrated on the production of wine labels, posters, and reproductions of paintings. The finely developed skills of its lithographic craftsmen combined with the subtle chemistry of lithography could do what the camera could not, and after World War II this catalytic mixture was to be placed at the service of Braque, Chagall, and Picasso. Those artists, finding the shop, its *patron*, and its craftsmen all willing and able to support and sustain their creative efforts, went beyond the mere repetition of their studio work and thereby revived a medium too long dormant.

The postwar interest in these three artists by members of the educated middle class and the economic situation that gave them extra money for luxuries opened the market for artist's prints to an extent never before experienced. The lithographs printed at Mourlot in their inexpensive version as exhibition posters and in the more costly signed and limited editions were available for purchase in America as well as Europe. As the number of collectors of modern prints grew after the war so the number of artists who turned to printmaking increased. The artist whose appeal carried beyond the *aficionados* of French modern prints was Marc Chagall.

After his short stay in 1922–23 in Germany, where he created his first prints, Chagall moved back to Paris. (He had lived in Paris from 1910 to 1914, returning to Russia to participate in various cultural undertakings by the new government after 1917 and leaving in 1922.) In Paris he painted prodigiously and produced many prints, mostly for Vollard's book-publishing ventures. His *Self Portrait with Grimace* (1924–25) shows the style of etching and aquatint that he utilized for his hundreds of plates for *Dead Souls*, *The Fables of La Fontaine*, and *The Bible*. Vollard had attempted in 1927 to have Chagall work on plates photoengraved from his gouaches, particularly toward the end of making color prints. Although this method served Rouault well (even though he complained that more work was expended on obliterating the photoengraving than in using it), Chagall's work did not photograph properly, and he ended up transcribing the essentials

80

80 Marc Chagall (1889–1985), *Self Portrait with Grimace*, 1924–25. Etching and aquatint, 14$\frac{11}{16}$ × 10$\frac{3}{4}$ (37 × 27·3). Gift of the artist

of each composition to plates and working freely upon them. The enormous quantity of etchings of the 1930s, whose literal scenes have been made more palpable by Chagall's original inventiveness, are very deft and direct narrative renderings. Chagall used aquatint as a pale wash underlying and often disappearing behind myriads of rapid strokes of the etching needle. However immediate the result appears, Chagall's etchings are the culmination of many trials which prepared the plate for its final ingenuous appearance in print.

Chagall made only a few lithographs and woodcuts during the 1920s and none during the 1930s. Like his etchings (and most of the prints created in the 1920s) they were black and white. Not until Chagall's exile in the U.S.A. during World War II did he have the right conjunction of commission, craftsman, and time to produce color prints. While the illustrations to four tales from the *Arabian Nights* 88 (New York, Pantheon, 1948) are brilliant in color and contain much of the fanciful mystery of Chagall's paintings, they are basically translations of gouaches made by a technically superb craftsman, Albert Carman. The tones are built up in the manner of photographic color process, using a set of basic tones to which Chagall added a few accents of strong color. More important than the rather impersonal

93

technique, however, was the appearance at long last of color prints by
an artist whose work was attaining the dazzle of a mythical mountain of
jewels. The appeal of both his unbridled use of color and his widely
accepted subject-matter insured for Chagall an audience far beyond
that of any of his contemporaries. He returned to Paris in 1948. Two
years later he began to work with Charles Sorlier at the workshop of
Fernand Mourlot. Throughout the 1950s and 1960s Chagall's lithographs poured from Mourlot's shop; Paris was deluged with bouquets,
the circus merrily rang, and representations of Old and New Testament
subjects became, in their printed form, icons in the homes and offices
of the postwar bourgeoisie.

Chagall, of course, was not the only former avant-garde artist to
find enthusiastic acceptance by the establishment. As his subject-
matter became increasingly intelligible to those who sought romantic
impact from what they viewed, so Chagall's work prevailed. The
scintillating harbor and race-course scenes with which Raoul Dufy

81 *(left)* Raoul Dufy (1877–1953),
plate 4 from *La Mer*. Paris, L'Etoile,
1925. Lithograph, 14⅛ × 18½
(35·8 × 47). Purchase Fund

82 Pierre Bonnard (1867–1947),
plate 13 from *Dingo*. Paris, Vollard,
1924. Etching, page 14⅝ × 11
(37 × 28). Louis E. Stern Collection

replaced his heavier folk-art style also eventually appealed to those
segments of French society who liked to see the places they frequented
become glorified in art. Dufy's series of views of the Marseilles harbor
of 1925 are among the few color lithographs of the 1920s. They share
with Matisse's work of the period a quick-sketch quality primarily
achieved by the deft management of the lithographic crayon. However, the decorative nature of the style of execution is further embellished by Dufy with an inevitable whimsy that compromises the
daringly free action of his line and color.

    André Derain, another of the former Fauves, turned, as did Picasso
and Braque, to classical art after World War I. His series of lithographic
portraits of the late 1920s appear monumental in scale because of their
strong sculptural structure. They also have the languorous disposition
of Matisse's nudes of a few years earlier. Completely separate from this
later tendency of Derain were his illustrations for Rabelais's *Pantagruel*
(Paris, Albert Skira, 1943) consisting of 179 color woodcuts. Returning

81

91

to motifs derived from folk art or European primitive sources, Derain created a volume illuminated with flat, simplified forms that were composed into playing-card figures, landscapes, flowers, and other embellishments. Derain worked with Roger Lacourière (the latter's first venture away from the etching and engraving procedures) for several years, carving the wood blocks and evolving the color selections which were used to print each composition with one inking only. The uneven coverage of the color was due to the hand application of each tone. Derain had wished to model his illustrations after some of the earliest woodcuts, those used for playing cards in the fifteenth century. Instead of coloring the finished print by hand, as was customary with the earliest woodcuts, Derain quixotically colored the blocks before printing.

Pierre Bonnard, whose lithographs for *Parallèlement* began this history of twentieth-century printmaking, continued to illustrate books with prints well into the 1940s. His first etchings, for Octave Mirbeau's *Dingo* (Paris, Ambroise Vollard, 1924), charmingly *82* delineate the rather pedestrian tale of a dog's life. Throughout the book the illustrations mirror the community that approved of and acquired the sunny, lighthearted paintings by Bonnard and older French artists.

Another, but younger, artist whose work appealed in the same way was the Bulgarian Jules Pascin, who arrived in Paris around 1905. Like Bonnard's, his work had a personal style that, remaining representational, did not repel or cause the confusion engendered by the creations of the avant-garde. His color etchings for Charles Perrault's *92* *Cinderella* (*Cendrillon*, Paris, M.-P. Trémois, 1929) are among the most delicate and ethereal prints of this century. Pascin's line-and-smudge technique is sensitively adapted by the utilization of soft-ground, which disperses all sharp edges and retains the effect of pastel and soft pencil. Pascin created many etchings and lithographs, mainly of nude figures, but never surpassed his magical Cinderella before his suicide in 1930.

The sculptor Aristide Maillol was the master of the nude figure. His career, like Bonnard's, began in the 1890s with the Nabis and continued into the 1940s. His twentieth-century work in prints was also mainly book illustration. His first works were for Count Harry Kessler, who had established his own press in Weimar in 1913. The books, designed by Englishmen, were based upon the ideas of the

83 Georges Rouault (1871–1958), *The Little Dwarf*, plate 4 from *Cirque de l'Etoile Filante*. Paris, Vollard, 1938. Aquatint, $12\frac{1}{8} \times 8\frac{5}{16}$ (30.8 × 21). Gift of the artist

nineteenth-century reviver of book art, William Morris. Maillol

84 began his woodcuts for Kessler's *Virgil* in 1912, but because of delays caused by the war, the first volume did not appear until 1926. Maillol and his nephew, Gaspard, developed the paper for this volume in Montval. The simple woodcuts, which Maillol cut himself, are extremely harmonious with the text, and still embody the plastic strength and tension of a sculptor's work. Maillol continued to make woodcuts for classical texts until his death in 1944.

If one were to examine only French references to prints of this period, one would have to accept André Dunoyer de Segonzac as the most prominent etcher of his time. He began with a tendency to emulate the mannerisms of the lesser Cubists in his etched illustrations to Tristan Bernard's *Tableau de Boxe* (Paris, Nouvelle Revue, 1922),

alia serpullumque herbas contundit olentis.
at mecum raucis, tua dum vestigia lustro,
sole sub ardenti resonant arbusta cicadis.
nonne fuit satius tristis Amaryllidos iras
atque superba pati fastidia, nonne Menalcan,
quamvis ille niger, quamvis tu candidus esses?
o formose puer nimium ne crede colori!
alba ligustra cadunt, vaccinia nigra leguntur.
despectus tibi sum, nec qui sim quaeris Alexi,
quam dives pecoris, nivei quam lactis abundans:
mille meae Siculis errant in montibus agnae;
lac mihi non aestate novom, non frigore defit.
canto, quae solitus, siquando armenta vocabat,

16

84 Aristide Maillol (1861–1944), page 16 from *Eclogues* by Virgil. London, Walker for Cranach Press, 1927. Woodcut, page 12¾ × 9⅞ (32·4 × 25). Henry Church Fund

85 André Dunoyer de Segonzac
(1884–1974), *Portrait of Colette*,
1932. Etching, 9⅛ × 8¼ (23 × 21).
Gift of Peter H. Deitsch

which have much in common with Jacques Villon's figurative prints of 1909. Like Villon, Segonzac was an exceptionally talented maker of prints, and his understanding of what etched lines can do is nowhere more apparent than in his portrait of the author who depicted French society of the period so succinctly, *Colette* (1932). Segonzac, too, was a servant to the zeal of Ambroise Vollard, and devoted nearly twenty years to etching 300 plates, 119 of which were to decorate *The Georgics* of Virgil (Paris, the artist, 1944[47]), published after Vollard's death. It was Vollard's attraction to Segonzac's illustrations for a book by Colette that inspired him to ask for another of the same combination. The artist preferred to reveal his childhood love of the French countryside beside the text of Virgil. The period was a fruitful one for reminiscence (it was the height of provincialism in countries where art had not yet fully blossomed), and Segonzac's return to landscape and particularly man's use of the open land was only typical of a world-wide trend. During the 1920s both Maurice de Vlaminck and Maurice Utrillo savored the rewards of their earlier notoriety by producing landscapes and cityscapes, mostly in the form of transfer lithographs. Vlaminck had shown both verve and skill in his earlier expressive

85

88 Marc Chagall (1889–1985), plate XII from *Arabian Nights*. New York, Pantheon, 1948. Lithograph, $14\frac{7}{8} \times 11\frac{3}{8}$ (37.8 × 28.9). Louis E. Stern Collection

86 (*top left*) Henri Matisse (1869–1954), *Horse, Rider and Clown* from *Jazz*. Paris, Tériade, 1947. Pochoir, sheet $16\frac{1}{4} \times 25\frac{1}{4}$ (41.2 × 64). Gift of the artist

87 (*left*) Georges Braque (1882–1963), *Varnished Chariot (Chariot III)*, 1955. Embossed lithograph, $12\frac{5}{8} \times 16\frac{5}{8}$ (32 × 42.2). Gift in honor of René d'Harnoncourt

woodcuts, while Utrillo had never evinced an interest in printmaking before he achieved fame. The *raison d'être* of the later prints by these two artists became the basis for the many arguments that arose from those who decried the commercialism of printmaking.

How sensitive and remarkable an artist's print could be, and yet have the most ordinary subject-matter, can be seen in the etchings of the Italian painter Giorgio Morandi. Morandi concentrated exclusively on two subjects: the landscape around his native Bologna and the still life. Early in his artistic career, he had been an admirer of de Chirico and Carrà, and at that time produced still lifes with unexpected accumulations of objects and implausible shadows emanating from them. In the 1920s he dropped this pseudoreality for a far more sensitive examination of form, turning boxes, vases, and other containers this way and that to find the myriad possibilities in still life. His still lifes have been compared to Renaissance paintings depicting the towers of San Gimignano, and it is evident that artists like Piero della Francesca and Paolo Uccello contributed to Morandi's develop-

89 Giorgio Morandi (1890–1964), *Still Life with Coffee Pot*, 1933. Etching, 11 11/16 × 15 3/8 (29·7 × 39). Louise R. Smith Fund

90 Fernand Léger (1881–1955), *The Vase*, 1927. Lithograph, 20$\frac{15}{16}$ × 17$\frac{1}{16}$ (53 × 43·3). Gift of Abby Aldrich Rockefeller

ment. His landscapes also partake of a strong sense of planar activity, while still representational to the point of exact identification. As an etcher, Morandi was the modern equivalent of the earliest Italian etcher, Parmigiano, and like him used the etching needle to produce networks of tones and shadows that trapped the sharp white of the   *89* paper, filtering it or heightening it as he desired.

    To return to the French artists of the earliest generation of twentieth-century moderns, Fernand Léger was the carrier of the Cubist strain as it developed into objectively composed abstract art. His tubular human formations in the teens and early 1920s and his predominantly geometrical compositions in the late 1920s inspired many younger artists. They were to combine his sense of solid form with the architectural structuralism of the De Stijl and Bauhaus artists, and become the dominant school of painting during the 1930s. Léger's earliest color lithograph, *The Vase* (*Abstraction Still Life*, 1927), is the corner-   *90* stone for an entire decade of art that wavered between objective abstraction and subjective Surrealism. In Léger's print a rigid pattern

91 André Derain (1880–
1954), page 24 from
Pantagruel by Rabelais.
Paris, Skira, 1943.
Woodcut, page $13\frac{9}{16} \times 11$
(34·4 × 28). Louis E. Stern
Collection

of straight lines is softened by the curved outlines of the vase and the
abstracted form of a filmstrip.

In 1931 Léger made his first visit to the U.S.A., reporting his
impressions to his French colleagues in the magazine *Cahiers d'Art*.
During the war he spent a very fertile period in the U.S.A., where he
traveled widely and painted 'better than I had ever painted before.' [22]
After he returned to Paris in 1946, he commenced his most important
printed project, the vibrant lithographs and text of *Cirque* (Páris,
Tériade, 1950). Distilling his memories of the great American circus
of Barnum and Bailey, Léger wrote in *Cirque*, 'In the "Barnum" with

94

92 Jules Pascin (Julius
Pincas) (1885–1930),
plate 1 from *Cendrillon* by
Charles Perrault. Paris,
Trémois, 1929. Etching,
page 18 × 12½ (45·7 × 38).
Louis E. Stern Collection

its three rings at Madison Square Garden, forty acrobats go through
their act forty metres up. If one falls the music gets louder, making it
more intense, the lights are moved, and while he tumbles down into
the void, you are already looking at the following attraction in
another ring.'[23] The lithograph illustrating this text is not the most
vivid in color but does show the manner in which Léger floated patches
of color behind his lines and shapes of black, disassociating them from
any previously meaningful function and allowing the viewer to
determine their relationship to the recognizable shapes outlined in
black.

Because of his attitude toward his twentieth-century environment and his decision to select many of his subjects and forms from the industrial world, Léger's post-Cubist work had a vital effect on younger artists. He had a profound understanding of the new visual properties of film and was able to utilize film, both in creating a cinema (*Ballet Mécanique* and others) which examined objects in specific time sequences and in creating compositions that were segmented into film frames or emphasized the concept of camera focus, especially the close-up. Léger's work appealed to several American artists who sought the ephemeral infusion of inspiration in Paris. Foremost among these was Stuart Davis, who had matured in the aftermath of the influential Armory Show (1913) in New York (see p. 122). He was to call Léger 'the most American painter painting today' [24] and Davis's own work depends on the way Léger interpreted the machine-made urban scene. In *Sixth Avenue El* (1931) Davis sets forth the manifold incidents and objects of the city streets within an abstract format. Davis, and later artists who chose this area of objective abstraction, were not only indebted to Léger, but could not escape the influence of Pablo Picasso.

93

93 Stuart Davis (1894–1964), *Sixth Avenue El*, 1931. Lithograph, 12 × 18 (30·4 × 45·7). Gift of Abby Aldrich Rockefeller

7   Picasso after Cubism

UNTIL THE LATE 1920s Picasso was, at best, a spasmodic printmaker. After his Cubist prints, most of which were book illustrations, projects that intruded upon the time he could devote to painting became many and varied. He designed scenery for Diaghilev's Ballets Russes, executed many portraits of his friends in an exaggerated realistic style, married and had a son, made his first lithograph (for an exhibition invitation at Paul Rosenberg's gallery in Paris), and began the annual sojourns at the seaside that characterized his life until 1948.

Apollinaire, who had been the first to use the term 'Surrealism,' died two days before the Armistice was declared (9 November 1918). The writers of the Surrealist movement that emerged in Paris around 1924 embraced several aspects of Picasso's earlier work that particularly appealed to them. André Breton rediscovered the momentous painting of 1907, *Les Demoiselles d'Avignon*, and published it for the first time in 1925 in *La Révolution Surréaliste*.[25] While the Surrealists sought to reveal the subconscious in their writings and paintings, they also believed that Picasso's Cubist works likewise revealed an unexposed part of life. This acceptance eventually led to a rather undefined relationship between Picasso and the Surrealist writers during the 1930s. One of the most important decisions during this relationship was the selection of the Minotaur as the symbol for a Surrealist publication and Picasso's illustration of this man-beast for the cover (*Minotaur*, 1933).

Picasso's work of the 1920s included still lifes that evolved from Cubism and human representations in a massive but refined classical mode. His feeling of being fettered to his increasingly bourgeois-like marriage erupted in violent and distorted forms at the end of the decade. The variety of subjects and techniques Picasso brought to his art in these years eventually took the form of prints. Classical motifs

94 Fernand Léger (1881–1955), page 51 from *Cirque*. Paris, Tériade, 1950. Lithograph, page 16⅝ × 12⅝ (42·2 × 32). Louis E. Stern Collection

dominated the prints of this period, beginning with an album of four transfer lithographs in 1924 and continuing with two volumes illustrated with etchings: Honoré de Balzac's *Le Chef d'œuvre inconnu* and Ovid's *Metamorphoses*. The young Albert Skira, who hoped to emulate the brilliant publisher Ambroise Vollard, commissioned the Ovid. The subjects allowed Picasso to run the classical gamut from divine nudes to raging horses. Vollard's choice of Balzac's tale about a painter's quest for the absolute gave Picasso the opportunity to relate the subject to his own dilemma. The artist works at his easel, creating in front of reality an image that, in its thorough confusion, is all reality.

In debt to Vollard for several paintings he had acquired, Picasso agreed to pay him with 100 of a group of etchings on which he was working. The so-called 'Vollard suite' was based on a combination of the two subjects of the previous illustrated books: mythology and the artist in his studio. As it was during this period (1931–35) that Picasso worked as a sculptor in Boisgeloup, his choice of subject was

108

the sculptor in his studio surrounded by models and statuary, generally of a classical nature. The revels in the studio included Minotaurs, and as the fertile subject evolved into dozens of plates, the amorous adventures of the sculptor became orgiastic. Then, abruptly, the bull-fight and other potent Mediterranean symbolic elements erupted into an idyllic sequence: the Minotaur falls in ritualistic battle, a child leads the blinded Minotaur, a woman bullfighter is thrown over the back of a gored horse. The culminating print of this explosion of terror was not part of the 100 etchings, but is the most important plate Picasso ever executed, the *Minotauromachy*. Here the Minotaur is confronted   96
by the child who now holds a candle to blind rather than lead the man-beast. They are separated by the cruel spectacle of a woman bullfighter tossed by a disemboweled horse. To the left is a man escaping up a lad-der, while, above, the scene is viewed by two women at a window ledge upon which two doves are strutting. In the far distance there is a boat – the escaping Theseus of the original tale of the Minotaur, perhaps. The entire composition brings together so much of Picasso's iconography that, more than any other of his works except the

95 Pablo Picasso (1881–1973), plate 4 from *Le Chef d'œuvre inconnu* by Honoré de Balzac. Paris, Vollard, 1931. Etching, 7⅝ × 11¾ (19·4 × 29). Louis E. Stern Collection

Guernica painting (1937), which was so closely based upon it, *Minotauromachy* has been subjected to considerable interpretation. While the Surrealists, by introducing dream symbols into their art, revived the critical art of conjecture, Picasso was to concentrate upon mythological and historical subjects, selecting those that inspired him to manipulate them for his own fulfillment.

The last prints of Picasso's indebtedness to Vollard include one composition, a *Faun Unveiling a Sleeping Woman*, that welds the mythology of Greeks with the Christian formalism of a Renaissance Annunciation. The faun enters a loggia, the light streaming in behind him. He raises the curtain with one hand allowing the light to fall upon the unsuspecting sleeper, thus creating a scene of great dramatic effect.

It was Roger Lacourière and his gifted associate Jacques Frélaut who introduced Picasso to some of the intricacies of intaglio printmaking in 1936. The sugar-lift process was the most painterly method, outside of lithography, of executing a print, and Picasso used this method for the last Vollard plates, as well as for thirty-one plates

96 Pablo Picasso (1881–1973), *Minotauromachy*, 1935. Etching, $19\frac{1}{2} \times 27\frac{7}{16}$ ($49 \cdot 5 \times 69 \cdot 7$). Purchase Fund

97 Pablo Picasso (1881–1973), *Faun Unveiling a Sleeping Woman*, 1936. Etching and aquatint, $12\frac{7}{16} \times 16\frac{7}{16}$ ($31 \cdot 6 \times 41 \cdot 7$). Purchase

illustrating selections from Buffon's *Histoire Naturelle* (published by Martin Fabiani in 1942 but commissioned by Vollard before his death). With a brush and a liquid containing sugar, Picasso drew on a copper plate, which was then covered with an impervious thin varnish or asphalt ground that, during the etching period, would prevent acid attacking portions of the plate not to be etched. After immersion in water the sugar would dislodge the ground over it, allowing those drawn areas to be etched. For the most part, resin was sprinkled over the open areas in order to obtain an aquatint texture rather than the harsher tone of simple open-bite etching.

It was with the sugar-lift method that Picasso created in 1939 his first color prints, portraits of Dora Maar that exist in only one or two examples. Work on these prints, which were to illustrate an auto-biography, ended abruptly when Picasso found he could paint with

the printing inks. He did, however, execute his largest print up to
that time, *Dancer with Tambourine* (1938). This was one of the few
prints that included Picasso's unique rearrangement and simultaneity
of focus on anatomical relationships that characterized his work of
the late 1930s. The three-quarters turn of the body in space, accomplished through depiction of several views containing familiar
contours, is given additional impetus by the ribbon-like execution
of the arms. Distortion and invention combine effectively to create the
appearance of rhythmic movement.

98

98 Pablo Picasso (1881–1973), *Dancer with Tambourine*, 1938. Etching and aquatint,
26¼ × 20⅛ (66·7 × 51). Acquired through the Lillie P. Bliss Bequest

99 Pablo Picasso (1881–1973), *Woman in an Armchair No. I*, 1949. Lithograph, $27\frac{3}{16} \times 20\frac{1}{8}$ (69 × 51). Curt Valentin Bequest

As he grew older the portraits of his mistresses, children, and friends were often transformed by ancient costumes and classical poses. This superimposition of the past upon contemporary lives lent a fictional quality to Picasso's work. In the style of a royal portrait of the seventeenth century, Picasso's lithographed *Woman in an Armchair* (1949) is a representation of Françoise Gilot in a Polish coat with embroidery on the arms. Executed the same year as his first color lithographs, this work was to have been in color. The fact that in order to make a lithograph in more than one color a separate stone is needed for each additional color led Picasso to redraw the subject several times. Eventually the artist found the additional stones more interesting in black than in a mix of color. It is quite likely that the few color lithographs he did finish were left more in the competent hands of Fernand Mourlot and his printers than produced from the very tedious process followed by printmakers.

Picasso's association with Mourlot after World War II marked a major moment in the revival of a medium. Before World War II Picasso's encounters with lithography had been minimal, usually in transfer drawings that barely touched the potential of the medium.

Indeed, lithography, which had flourished in full color during the 1890s, remained the printing medium of those of an older tradition (Bonnard and Matisse) and of those whose utilization of free gesture encouraged the use of crayon and *tusche* (the German Expressionists). Nevertheless, the medium, far younger and therefore considered more commercial than engraving and etching, had rarely been exploited for its potential subtleties since the 1890s. Picasso was to challenge lithography with his intense and constant probing. He demanded that the stones carry his images exactly as he wanted them, so ways were found to manipulate the entire chemical and printing processes. Although the images no longer challenged so fiercely the credence of the lay public, they continued to turn life this way and that, to discover for those who deigned to look (and for the first time, perhaps, there were more who wanted to possess these prints than there were prints available) the infinite ways of representing life.

One of the possibilities in lithography that Picasso found most enticing was the retention of the successive stages of his compositions. For those whose curiosity or scholarship begs to know how a work of art has evolved, no other process but printmaking requires that a record in the form of trial proofs be taken of each stage in the development of a composition. In lithography Picasso found that his crayon drawings on stone could be changed radically. His eleven variations of *The Bull*, beginning with a realistically rendered animal and ending with a linear one, and his *Two Nude Figures*, in which the watching and sleeping women exchanged identities as Picasso changed mistresses during the period he drew the eighteen states, are examples of Picasso's prodigious manner of creating images. In later years he was to retain every line and even cover mistakes with the scratched lines of frustration when moving from one composition to the next. Only in his early postwar lithographs did he reveal the complex decision-making process of the most artistically creative mind of the twentieth century.

After moving to the south of France Picasso found it increasingly difficult to continue making lithographs. Without a press at hand he had to wait for proofs to be sent from Paris. Ever the impetuous worker, these delays required a patience he did not possess. Then, having begun to make pottery in Vallauris, he was asked to make a poster by a local printer, Arnerá. Arnerá printed linoleum cuts, and Picasso made several linocut posters before he trapped himself into attacking the medium with more seriousness. His *Portrait of a Girl (after Cranach the Younger)* (1958) was an attempt to produce a multi-color print in the normal manner – one block for each color – but the colors did not print precisely. Picasso did not have the temperament for this tedious procedure. He therefore set out to make multicolor prints by using only one block, printing each color as he cut away more of the block. (It is possible that Arnerá utilized this system for its inherent economy in his own commercial linoleum cuts.) From the artist's point of view, this was naturally a far more challenging and risky manner of working.

Still Life under a Lamp (1962) is the most brilliant example of Picasso's one-block linoleum cuts. It represents well, too, the highly decorative turn his vision took in his last decade. This print, created when he was eighty years old, combines a youthful energetic sweep of line and color with an older nostalgia for quaint patterns. It is, altogether, a satisfying blend. This exceptional use of the rather lifeless linoleum vivifies the layers of flat unmodulated color and allows the exposed paper to become the source of light. *100*

Throughout his career, Picasso's superb draftsmanship served many subjects. His father taught him the importance of drawing, which thereafter was the dominant occupation of his life. From his earliest years he filled all available surfaces with instant sketches. There are thousands who possess menus, paper money, café napkins, and books of every sort with the special sketches that Picasso made within a matter of seconds especially for them. For Picasso drawing was a natural function that only death could halt. In his later years, after he had moved to the south of France and had fewer diversions, he filled hours between painting, sculpting, and pottery-making with drawing. Long series of compositions such as the 180 drawings he did in 1953–54, published as 'Picasso and the Human Comedy,' became an integral part of his later life. Almost entirely devoted to his now traditional subjects – the artist at work and play, the circus, the bullfight, and woman – Picasso drew with pencil, pen, felt pen, and the tools of the etcher and engraver.

In the late 1960s the artist could often be found in the middle of a maelstrom of copper plates and two concerned printers, the Crommelynck brothers. Emotional crises and loneliness had many times in the past forced Picasso to embark on projects that required highly concentrated effort and produced an exceptional quantity of works.

100 Pablo Picasso (1881–1973), *Still Life under a Lamp*, 1962. Linoleum cut, 20⅞ × 25¼ (53 × 64). Gift of Mrs. Donald B. Straus

Periodically, as he aged, traumatic events caused him to produce yet another large series of drawings. Certainly the death in 1968 of one of his closest and oldest friends, Jaime Sabartés, affected him profoundly, and the result of this emotional event was a series of 347 plates, etched, engraved and aquatinted from March to October. Picasso's traditional subjects prevail, although the disguises of the participants change. Swashbuckling, plume-hatted gentlemen of the period of Velázquez, playing sexually aggressive roles, seem to be an extremely sympathetic disguise for the aged Picasso. He devised ways for younger, rather dilettante, noblemen to participate with voluptuously nude women in explicitly detailed sexual acts while the old king, deprived of his own prowess, appeared as a voyeur.

116

While the sex-act prints of the '347' series assured its notoriety, they were neither Picasso's first nor last erotic compositions. How could the foremost observer of women in his time fail to show as many aspects of her being as he could record? In his prints alone, women are not only shown being admired and fondled, but also chased and bedded. The public nature of prints undoubtedly contributed, in the earlier works, to a disingenuous approach to the erotic. In his last prints his humorous vision of the sexual act was a sly wink at the broadening public attitude toward the erotic during the late 1960s.

Typical of the great quantity of etchings Picasso executed in the final decade of his life are the illustrations to the play *Le Cocu Magnifique* (Paris, Crommelynck, 1968) by Fernand Crommelynck. The plates were made about a year before the '347,' and many of the subjects are identical. Whereas in the '347' the pursuer of ladies is most often a mustachioed Spanish grandee, the male figure in this illustration is one of the most sensitively modeled and sympathetic characters in Picasso's late work. The female nude is rendered in the rushed scrapes that not only express the distressed flight of the pursued, but also give her the vaguely defined appearance of the intangible.

101

101 Pablo Picasso (1881–1973), plate 12 from *Le Cocu Magnifique* by Fernand Crommelynck. Paris, Crommelynck, 1968. Etching, $8\frac{3}{4} \times 12\frac{5}{8}$ (22·2 × 32). Monroe Wheeler Fund

Picasso's placement in the history of twentieth-century art depends entirely upon the point of view taken. There is no argument that the development of Cubism was his fundamental contribution that permanently affected future artistic expression. His imaginative use of materials, particularly in sculpture, not only broadened his impact upon the artistic community but encouraged a freer mode of approaching all media. After his Surrealist experiments, Picasso's imagery became, for some, mere embellishment upon earlier innovations. It is apparent that he did not communicate in his work any recognition of the changed environment of mid-twentieth-century France, nor any effect of the several new philosophical attitudes that were prevalent. His attachment to the Communist Party after the war was a position that, although Picasso felt sincerely sympathetic to its causes and goals, could not be resolved in his art. And yet his notoriety as an innovator continued throughout his life, his name was a household word in countries where his work had never been exhibited, and even the young, experimental artist could not and would not pretend to ignore Picasso.

In the area of his printmaking, Picasso followed a more conservative path than in other media, but his attitude toward the making of prints was exceptionally important to the future of the printed image. In the 1940s he took photoengravings of his own drawings and etched into them new elements, later printing them as both relief and intaglio prints. Rather than consciously search for new ways to make prints, he created images that expanded the possibilities of the print media. The quantity of these printed images (more than 1,900 compositions in editions from 25 to 150) substantiate the importance of printmaking in Picasso's creative life and should be seen as perhaps the most consequential production by any fine artist, whatever the medium. While Daumier created more prints, they did not have the breadth of imagery of Picasso's work, nor were they executed concurrently with an exceptional number of paintings and sculptures. Lastly, and as with the best artist-printmakers of the past, Picasso's prints have had considerable influence upon the artists of his time. The easy availability of prints has made them subjects of constant study and discussion, even from the time of Rembrandt. Through his prints Picasso has encouraged access to the print media by artists of all esthetic persuasions, thus further expanding their own potential influence.

8 Between the wars: Mexico, the United States, Japan

As HAS BEEN NOTED above, French art during the 1920s and 1930s was divided between the avant-garde and the establishment. The ideas of the avant-garde in Europe – from Moscow to Paris – were embraced by the more courageous young artists who fled from the relatively conservative tastes of their own countries, particularly those in the Western Hemisphere and other isolated areas. The artists who returned to their native lands after their experiences in the European maelstrom of unfettered creative freedom were often unable to sustain their commitment to avant-garde ideals. They had to deal with the realities of their own societies which, more often than not, were in political and economic turmoil, or lacked the combination of maturity and intellectual curiosity to sustain an advanced artistic movement.

A typical situation occurred in Mexico in the beginning of the 1920s. Diego Rivera had been working in Europe when he and other Mexican artists were recalled by their government to participate in the educational and cultural activities that would lead to an increase in national pride based on awareness of the virtues of the people and their past. The indigenous movement in Mexico had its equivalents in the regional art of the U.S.A. and the Social Realism of the Soviet Union. In each of these cases the pictorial works that were produced were meant to be seen and appreciated by the masses. Naturally, one of the foremost means of accomplishing the widest distribution of the social message in art was through the print media. The vast numbers of posters created by artists cannot be treated here, but some of their prints did have the staying power found in Daumier's pungent lithographs.

In Mexico the progenitor of the indigenous movement was the popular graphic artist José Guadalupe Posada. In his metal cuts and

102 Ben Shahn (1898–1969), *Triple Dip*, 1952. Serigraph, hand-colored, 29⅛ × 21 (74 × 53.3). Abby Aldrich Rockefeller Fund

103 Diego Rivera (1886–1957), *Zapata*, 1932. Lithograph, 16¾₁₆ × 13⅛ (41 × 33·3). Gift of Abby Aldrich Rockefeller

104 David Alfaro Siqueiros (1898–1974), *Moisés Sáenz*, 1931. Lithograph, 21⅜ × 16⅛ (54·3 × 41). Inter-American Fund

relief etchings for political and religious broadsides of the early 1900s he combined centuries-old Spanish influences with Indian traditions that had been altered but not eradicated by European domination. The self-taught artist, whose haunting Calaveras (spirits of the dead depicted to celebrate All Souls Day) and amusing city folk set the stage for a more serious response to culture, was a significant influence on two of Mexico's three great masters of the first third of the century, Diego Rivera, José Clemente Orozco, and David Alfaro Siqueiros. All three made lithographs that recapitulated the subjects of their major artistic contribution, the creation of mammoth murals. The revolution that was to politicize Mexicans for several decades came in 1910, shortly before Posada's death. Thereafter, art was devoted to the struggles and achievements of the peasants and the unprivileged. One of the leaders of the peasants during the revolution, Emiliano Zapata, appears prominently in the works of most Mexican artists, and Rivera's lithograph depicting him is perhaps the best-known print to emanate from Mexico. Rivera's European training is only vaguely apparent, and in his arrangement of figures he blends

103

121

incompletely digested modern spatial concepts with a personal interpretation of Pre-Columbian plastic representation.

Closer to the indigenous ancient forms is Siqueiros's portrait of the
104 Mexican educator *Moisés Sáenz* (1931). His monumental head rests
on the page in much the same manner as the large stone Olmec
heads sit upon the ground. Siqueiros was the most politically active of
the three artists, spending several periods in prison, and he lived the
longest. He spent his last years executing a mural with large areas of
high relief, and he also created some extremely lyrical lithographs for
an elephantine volume of Pablo Neruda's *Poems from the Canto
General* (New York, Racolin Press, 1968).

Orozco was more moderate politically than either Rivera or
Siqueiros, and seems to have comprehended more sensitively the
nature of the peasant's life. The character of his murals in the eastern
U.S.A. had a telling influence upon American artists, who had little
experience of such grandiose forms of representation. Orozco
executed many of his lithographs in New York, and their availability
there as well as the enthusiastic acceptance of the Mexican artists in
New York appears to have helped set the stage for American artists
with similar artistic and social goals.

The 'Ashcan' school of painting in New York of the early 1900s
included one artist who put his ideas of depicting real life into prints:
105 John Sloan. His etchings of city folk living out their lives in tene-
ments, bars, and rainy streets were a continuation of a national genre
tradition with a slightly ironic twinge. The influential Armory Show
in New York, which introduced a larger public to the then current
European styles, took place in 1913. This event marked a certain
degree of polarization between those artists who felt strongly that the
various currents of European avant-gardism flowed in the right
direction, and those who felt they could develop a more suitably
American art. Realism for a fanatically realistic people became the
stronger direction. Sloan, Bellows, Burchfield, Marsh, and many
others explored the subject of man in the unfriendly environment of
the city. Another form of realism was one that had its antecedents in
106 European art. Edward Hopper was perhaps the strongest American
painter to create etchings of the peculiarly vast and lonely American
scene, in his representations of both the land and the people. The low
horizon that he chose and even his etching manner were conscious
evocations of Rembrandt. However, the result was unmistakably

105 John Sloan (1871–1951), *Night Windows*, 1910. Etching, $5\frac{1}{4} \times 6\frac{7}{8}$ (13·3 × 17·5). Gift of Abby Aldrich Rockefeller

106 Edward Hopper (1882–1967), *Night Shadows*, 1921. Etching, $6\frac{15}{16} \times 8\frac{3}{16}$ (17·6 × 20·8). Gift of Abby Aldrich Rockefeller

American, and though he admired 'the quality of a brooding silent interior in this vast city'[26] that Sloan obtained, it was Hopper who best caught the kernel of that mood in his prints in the early 1920s.

As the Depression hardened in the mid-1930s, regional art tended to dominate. Two artists of mid-America, Thomas Hart Benton and Grant Wood, were among many who focused a magnifying glass upon their country and its less sophisticated inhabitants. Like most of the 1930s artists who made prints, they utilized black and white lithography, and between them they sought an acceptable way to extol the virtues of 'the people' while, occasionally, cheerfully mocking them. Significantly, both were influential teachers who, with the far more propagandistic Mexican muralists, set the form for younger artists.

To alleviate some of the effects of the Depression the United States government established the Works Progress Administration in 1935. Under the W.P.A., the Federal Art Project provided work for many artists, who in the course of their association with the project created myriads of prints and many murals for public buildings. The Social Realists were thrown together with abstract artists, and some of the younger painters who had received their training from the regionalist artists were awakened to the possibilities of abstract art through their contacts with such artists as Stuart Davis and Hans Hofmann. Among the less mature Project artists were Jackson Pollock and Willem de Kooning, who were to become the first internationally acclaimed American painters. The actual work done on the Project, as in the case of most institutionalized art, was secondary to its long-range influences upon the later work of many of the artists who were able to continue their artistic careers because of it.

Of the Social Realists in the Federal Art Project, Ben Shahn was to become the best known. He had assisted Diego Rivera with the latter's controversial murals for Rockefeller Center in New York (1932–33), and went on to create murals in post offices throughout New York City. His realism was militant, in the Mexican tradition, and he rebelled against both the less politically sophisticated regionalists and the nonpolitical Abstractionists. The economic strain of the Depression had vitalized the political left, and Shahn was to use his art as a spotlight on the social injustice of his time. His combination of a unique calligraphic style with flat, poster-paint technique lent itself well to printmaking once the development of silkscreen as a medium took place. Shahn's first silkscreens (or 'serigraphs,' as they were called in an attempt to bring the commercial technique into the realm of art)[27] were made in 1941 and depicted poor immigrants and puppet-like politicians. His prints became well known after the war, when he had left his more volatile political themes behind and began to incorporate elements derived from the work of Paul Klee.

Shahn was the first artist to use silkscreen extensively. He began by trying to imitate the progressive building up of tone and volume that was characteristic of painting. Silkscreen was the one medium where this could be rather successfully accomplished, so it was inevitable that the early 1940s was also a period when many paintings by contemporary artists were reproduced in silkscreen. Silkscreen had many advantages which had developed through its demanding use as a commercial tool. Many colors could be laid down on paper in perfect alignment (registration). Because there were several methods of creating the image on the screen (with glue, cutting gelatin patterns, and various photographic techniques), these images could have the variety found in painting as well as an entirely new appearance.

Shahn was to drop the painterly approach he first used and to retain only linear elements, which he often hand-colored. Typical of these prints in which the black linear image is drawn directly upon the silkscreen and the color applied by hand to the sheet before the black is printed is *Triple Dip* (1952). Shahn complained that he could not obtain the richness he wanted through color printing, and although later artists were to achieve brilliantly colored prints with silkscreen, the glue-based paint tends to be extremely homogeneous and absorbs light to a great degree. The more transparent color that Shahn applied by brush had a greater vibrancy.

102

The silkscreen, developed by a small group of artists who were hardly in the mainstream of major artistic creation, was to become an important tool in art twenty-five years later. However, other seemingly unimportant occurrences in regional art all over the world likewise had later repercussions. The 1920s and 1930s were, after all, periods during which giant steps in international communication took place. In the face of so much more information about the rest of the world it now seems inevitable that even the artists in remote Japan would seek a way to express a new sensitivity to their own past.

The woodcut appears to have lost its status in Japan as a major form of artistic expression upon the death of the famous Ukiyo-e artist

Hiroshige in 1858. Today the aniline colors used in many of the prints made during Emperor Meiji's reign (1868–1912) have a gaudy character that makes one yearn for the comparatively subtle tones of the woodcuts of only a few decades earlier. It was the latter style that received such a warm welcome by artists in Paris in the second half of the nineteenth century. The woodcut became transformed from an artistic and sensitive depiction of fading tradition into a journalistic and commercial tool. The hiatus between the old and contemporary cultures created artistic chaos, for the new ways were Occidental and stressed a different hierarchy for art forms. Painting in the Western style became important, whereas the socially integrated forms like woodcuts, which depended on a complex scheme of artist and artisans filling a community's demands, fell completely outside the realm of the artist.

A few artists sought to place the woodcut in the mainstream of artistic expression. Kanae Yamamoto and Koshiro Onchi were foremost among those who took European woodcutting as a model in the early decades of the twentieth century. One of the artists who revived interest in ancient Japanese forms, particularly early Buddhist prints, was Un'ichi Hiratsuka. In the late 1920s he was among the first to combine the Western technique of direct cutting with a traditional Japanese spirit. One of his students was Shiko Munakata from Northern Honshu province, who was to go beyond earlier attempts to keep a tradition alive. In 1936 he became associated with the 'mingei' movement, which could be equated with the somewhat earlier regional movements in the West. 'Mingei' was an attempt to return to craftsmanship as practiced in the countryside, free of the commercial taint that had compromised the more sophisticated artists. The leader of the movement, Dr. Yanagi, recognized in Munakata's work the full meaning of 'mingei' he sought to instill in the young. Munakata's prints, filled with Japanese legend, Buddhist figures, and traditional images, are, like their counterparts in Mexico, hybrids of modern European influences and older national expression taken predominantly from folk and archaic sources. His forthright directness in attacking the wood block with the simple chisels used by children is similar to the approach of the German Expressionists, who sought not only to convey the emotion they felt when they carved their forms, but also to retain the character of the wood itself. This concept is in direct opposition to the Japanese tradition of

107

woodcut production, in which one person draws the composition, another cuts it from the block or blocks, and a third prints it. Munakata's method was characteristic, however, of peasant craftsmanship and carried with it a refreshing frankness long missing from the traditional woodcut.

107 Shiko Munakata (1903–1975), *Flower Hunting Mural*, 1954. Woodcut, $51\frac{7}{8} \times 62\frac{7}{8}$ ($131 \cdot 7 \times 159 \cdot 7$). Gift of the Felix and Helen Juda Foundation

9 Printmaking after World War II: the persistence of Expressionism and Surrealism

A POLITICAL DISPLACEMENT of artists began some years before World War II and the actual outbreak of hostilities. Hitler's determination to unify his people through mass hatred of minorities, particularly those involved in intellectual and creative pursuits, forced the closing of the Bauhaus in 1933, sending its artists into exile. Josef Albers was the first from the Bauhaus to go to the U.S.A. in 1931, and there he participated in an innovative form of education at Black Mountain College, North Carolina. Feininger returned to the U.S.A. in 1937. Klee moved to Switzerland and Kandinsky to Paris. All the German Expressionists and artists of the Neue Sachlichkeit found themselves considered degenerate by the Nazis. Beckmann spent the war years in Holland while Grosz went to the U.S.A. and even became a citizen (renouncing his citizenship upon his return to Germany shortly before his death in 1959). Kokoschka and Schwitters found refuge in Great Britain, where Schwitters died in 1948. By far the largest exodus, however, occurred when Hitler's army occupied France. It then became necessary for Marc Chagall, Jacques Lipchitz, and other Jewish artists to escape to a place where religious persecution would be less likely to occur. With Max Ernst, Fernand Léger, André Masson, Matta, and the major Surrealist writer, André Breton, they fled to New York. Miró returned to Spain. Only Braque, Matisse, and Picasso were able to remain in France with little disturbance from the occupying enemy.

While some illustrations by Picasso were published during the war, very few artists made prints during the occupation because of the lack of materials and skilled craftsmen. Perhaps the most seminal event in the history of twentieth-century printmaking was Stanley William Hayter's removal of his Atelier 17 from Paris to New York. As he considered himself a Surrealist (because he utilized automatism to create the basis of his compositions), his shop drew many of the Surrealist group to it. As they discussed their common problems (most felt extremely dislocated in the English-speaking community, where they could barely communicate), some of them executed a few prints. A few American artists joined in the discussions or were attracted to try their hand at Hayter's methods of intaglio print-making.

One of the Americans was Jackson Pollock. Before the war both he and his brother had made lithographs under the influence of the American regional artist Thomas Hart Benton. Pollock had already been introduced to the concept of automatism in the provocative paintings of Masson and Ernst shown in New York in 1942. It was noted that even Pollock's painting in 1942 'resembles Hayter in general whirling figures.' [28] In 1944 Pollock went to Atelier 17 and achieved through the method of automatism some of the first dynamic and expressive compositions that were to characterize the early mode of American Abstract Expressionism. In his etchings there are ele- *108* ments derived from the prewar compositions of Picasso, whose *Guernica* was a magnetic attraction at New York's Museum of Modern Art.

Pollock's Atelier 17 etchings remained unknown until William S. Lieberman and Pollock's widow found them in a warehouse. In 1967 six were posthumously published by his estate and Marlborough Galleries, New York. A proof of one of the larger plates communi-

108 Jackson Pollock (1912–1956), *Untitled 4*, 1945. Engraving and drypoint, $14\frac{3}{4} \times 17\frac{7}{8}$ (37·5 × 45·4). Gift of Mrs. Lee Krasner Pollock

cates the frenzy and pent-up emotion that so eloquently emerged in Pollock's drip paintings. Except for these few early proofs there are no significant prints by the major American artists working in the energetic abstract style during the 1940s and 1950s. Franz Kline had a drawing reproduced as an etching in *21 Etchings and Poems*, published in 1960; Willem de Kooning also had an etching in the same publication, which had been conceived in 1951 by members of New York's Atelier 17 and combined in each composition the poet's words and the artist's embellishment. Gorky, Hofmann, Rothko, and Still never created original prints in their mature styles.

Because the most vital Abstract Expressionist period, during the late 1940s and 1950s, was spent by artists in their studios or at places like the Club in New York expounding their theories, it was unlikely that there would be any movement to create prints. Hayter's methods encouraged artists to become printmakers, thus removing them somewhat from the dynamism of the new, fresh undertakings of the painters. Several artists who responded well to the craftsman orientation of Hayter's workshop created major works within the limitations of the intaglio medium. Three of the most important, Gabor Peterdi, Mauricio Lasansky, and Karl Schrag, all immigrants, dominated the field of printmaking in the U.S.A. throughout the 1950s.

All three were mature artists who utilized some, but not all, of Hayter's methods. Peterdi, a Hungarian, was profoundly interested *109* in the landscape and its nonhuman inhabitants. His *Germination* (1952), with its strata of living matter, is an excellent example of the complexity of intaglio technology of the period: it combines soft- and hard-ground etching, engraving, aquatint, and offset color. The overall patterning of the composition reflects the concurrent tendency in painting, but as in most of the printmaking in the U.S.A. during this period, the image seems of less importance than the means *110* used to obtain it. Schrag, from Karlsruhe, Germany, also made exceptional use of the materials at hand in Atelier 17, which he led after Hayter's return to Paris in 1950. Schrag brought to his plates an emotional approach that he shared with several other printmakers who worked primarily in wood, a particularly popular medium during the postwar revival of interest in the prints of the former *111* adversaries, Germany and Japan. Mauricio Lasansky never abandoned his interest in the figurative, already well developed before he left his home in Argentina in 1943. Hayter's fluid use of the burin was the

130

109 Gabor Peterdi (b.
1915), *Germination*, 1952.
Aquatint, etching and
engraving, $19\frac{3}{4} \times 23\frac{13}{16}$
(50 × 60·5). Gift of
Walter Bareiss

110 Karl Schrag (b. 1912), *Falling Night*, 1949. Etching and engraving, $17\frac{7}{8} \times 12$ (45·4 × 30·5).
Purchase Fund

111 Mauricio Lasansky (b. 1914), *Self Portrait*, 1957. Engraving, drypoint, roulette and
etching, $35\frac{5}{8} \times 20\frac{1}{2}$ (90·5 × 52). Inter-American Fund

basis for Lasansky's engraving technique, which allowed him to create intaglio prints on a larger scale. Figurative artists in the U.S.A. had a much wider audience than their abstract colleagues, and there was a loyal group of collectors who supported the efforts of those artists who found human representation basic to their visions of life in the post-atomic age. While Lasansky's presentation of the tormented human has its roots in a Hispanic tradition, one that formed a part of the foundation for Picasso's prints of the late 1930s, his new use of expanded scale reflected the emphasis on size in American painting. The presence in the U.S.A. of the major monumental painting of the twentieth century, the twenty-five-foot, eight-inch-wide *Guernica*, undoubtedly had some effect.

In printmaking one American artist made works that reached the size of most vertical paintings of the 1950s, Leonard Baskin. To do this he used large sheets of plywood to create giant figurative woodcuts. Baskin has an absolute sense of monumental scale which he has imposed upon grotesquely formed figures that consist of highly complex tangles of virtuoso woodcutting. *Man of Peace* (1952), a monument related to the Korean War, while not the largest of Baskin's woodcuts of this period (they won for him a first prize in the São Paulo Bienal in 1961), is the most successful manifestation of his and many other artists' attitudes toward both the formal and the philosophical problems of art in the 1950s.

Baskin was not, however, the only artist to work with the woodblock in the U.S.A. during the postwar decades. Among many competent woodcutters, the Uruguayan Antonio Frasconi has had few peers in this medium (one can think only of H. A. P. Grieshaber in Germany). By using the gouge in an Expressionist manner and retaining the texture of the woodblock, Frasconi has been able to capture an intensity in his subjects. Like many of the printmakers at the very political Taller de Grafica in Mexico City, Frasconi often uses the woodcut for social comment.

One younger American printmaker carried the art of the woodcut into new realms during the 1950s. Carol Summers, also using plywood sheets for his larger forms, created dynamic landscapes of unusual impact. By applying ink to the paper directly, using the cut wood as a limiting surface beneath, Summers obtained some of the brilliantly colored and liquid quality of watercolor, yet the total effect is entirely unique and mysterious in its own right.

113 Antonio Frasconi (b. 1919), *The Storm is Coming*, 1950. Woodcut, $22 \times 15\frac{1}{2}$ ($55 \cdot 8 \times 39 \cdot 3$) Inter-American Fund

112 Leonard Baskin (b. 1922), *Man of Peace*, 1952. Woodcut, $59\frac{1}{2} \times 30\frac{5}{8}$ ($151 \times 77 \cdot 7$). Purchase Fund

114 Carol Summers (b. 1925), *Monte Amiata*, 1958. Woodcut, $44\frac{1}{2} \times 35\frac{3}{4}$ ($113 \times 90 \cdot 8$). Gift of Mr. and Mrs. Peter A. Rübel

The split between painter and printmaker, perhaps precipitated by Hayter's students, who placed inordinate emphasis on the ingredients of printmaking, did not appear important until the American painters began to make prints. There was, after all, no market for these painters' prints, for beyond the interest in the very limited, hand-made prints by the intaglio and woodcut artists, the only prints worth owning came from the School of Paris in general, and Picasso in particular. Having been cut off so long from the heart of the art world, by both the war and the Depression, Americans were eager to use their new money and confidence in the formation of collections of European art. In such a climate the American abstract painters and sculptors found an adversary worth battling with their best efforts. Eventually their work found an international audience, too, and was recognized as a major artistic flowering. By the early 1960s a few American artists were invited to make lithographs in European print workshops, and the formula that created the print 'boom' of the 1960s was established.★

Sam Francis, a younger abstract painter from California, was the first to produce a significant group of prints in the Expressionist, or action, style of the American school. Since he spent most of the 1950s in Paris, he had some indication of how prints by major painters were accepted. His visit to Japan in 1957 accentuated his affinity with the *haboku*, or 'flung ink,' style of the Japanese. He began his first attempts in lithography in 1959 at Universal Limited Art Editions near New York City, but did not complete those prints until 1968. In 1960, in conjunction with creating a poster for an exhibition in Europe, he made a series of color lithographs with the Swiss printer Emil Matthieu. *The White Line* (1960) is one of the first prints that emphasize the differences between the American and European postwar abstract schools, for the latter artists either submitted their seemingly free gestural lines to a rigorous refining process (*i.e.*, Hartung and Soulages) or entrapped figurative elements in

143

★ It was during the 1950s that, in order to protect the print buyer, the question of originality as a criterion for judging the quality of a print was answered with a definition promulgated by the Print Council of America in *What Is an Original Print?* (1961). Not only did the definition aid the consumer, but it also tended to question the artist's integrity and his right to free expression. Inevitably many of the prints of the 1960s failed to conform to the definition and were considered repro-ductions.

115 Willem de Kooning (b. 1904), Untitled, 1960. Lithograph, $42\frac{3}{4} \times 30\frac{3}{4}$ (108·6 × 78). Gift of Mrs. Bliss Parkinson

116 Robert Motherwell (b. 1915), *In Black with Yellow Ochre*, 1963. Lithograph, 18⅛ × 13⅞ (46 × 35·2). Gift of the Celeste and Armand Bartos Foundation

117 Barnett Newman (1905–1970), Untitled, 1961. Lithograph, 13¾ × 9⅞ (35 × 25). Gift of Mr. and Mrs. Barnett Newman in honor of René d'Harnoncourt

emotionally activated linear webs (COBRAs), while Francis composed without preconceptions or restrictions. Here the flung drops of ink and amorphous squares compose themselves from the superimposition of five independently executed lithographic stones upon which Francis applied his drips and daubs. The resultant print has an excitement of immediacy unhampered by subject – other than the instantly apparent theme of color, movement, and surface.

The second artist to work in lithography, which appeared to be the ideal medium for the action painter, was Willem de Kooning. In California there were several artists who were interested in lithography and taught it at the University of California at Berkeley. One evening de Kooning was persuaded by them to make two prints *115* in the University's workshop. His large black and white untitled lithograph of 1960 successfully 'freezes' the bravado of the artist's stroke, the visualization in permanent form of the emotional core of action. While Francis periodically turned to lithography during the 1960s as a form of expression, de Kooning waited another decade

136

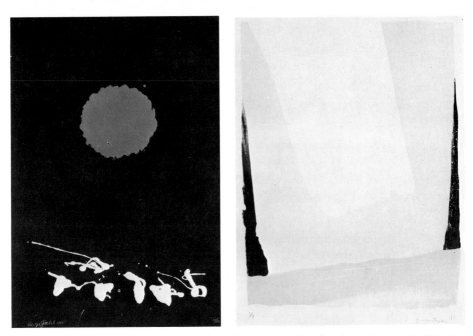

118 Adolph Gottlieb (1903–1974), *Black Ground – Red Disc*, 1966. Serigraph, 28¼ × 20 (71·7 × 50·8). Gift of Marlborough-Gerson Gallery

119 Helen Frankenthaler (b. 1928), *White Portal*, 1967. Lithograph, 19³⁄₁₆ × 14⅝ (48·7 × 37). Gift of the Celeste and Armand Bartos Foundation

before he put any amount of time into the creation of prints. By the 1970s he had again returned to figurative elements. The more than twenty lithographs issued in 1970 are vibrant with lively brush strokes that appear scattered haphazardly but evolve into landscapes and figures.

Robert Motherwell, during the war years, became a close associate of the European Surrealist refugees. He was one of the few Americans who exhibited with the Surrealists and, like Jackson Pollock, had his first one-man show at Peggy Guggenheim's Art of This Century Gallery, the center of avant-garde activity. He contributed a water-color to the Surrealist album *VVV* (1942), which also contained prints by Chagall, Masson, and Tanguy. Although he began to make etchings at Atelier 17 around 1942, and occasionally made a print during the 1950s, his direct Expressionist attack was most successfully applied in lithography. Motherwell made his first lithographs at Universal Limited Art Editions in 1961. *In Black with Yellow Ochre* 116 (1963) is a variation in print form on his most deeply felt theme, the

137

Spanish Civil War, upon which he has based many paintings, generally titled *Spanish Elegies*. Motherwell's broad and intense patches of black appear rarely in his prints, since during the 1960s his preoccupation was more directly with collage, economical attenuated lines, and large fields of color. The collages incorporating Gauloise cigarette packages were eventually introduced by Motherwell into etchings and serigraphs.

Other artists who have been categorized as Abstract Expressionists made prints during the 1960s. Barnett Newman, who was among the last of his generation to gain acceptance, made only a few prints. His 117 first works in 1961 at the Pratt Graphics Workshop in New York were black and white lithographs in his characteristic style of a monochromatic, relatively homogeneous plane interrupted by a single vertical strip or 'zip,' as Newman named this active element. His only prints that incorporated his special color sense formed part of an album titled *18 Cantos* (New York, Universal Limited Art Editions, 1964). These lithographs were meant to be seen together despite the dramatic changes of paper size (Newman attempted to resolve the conflict between the edge of the print and the margin by altering the spatial relationships between the printed area and the edge of the paper). Before his death in 1970 Newman made two black and white etchings almost entirely devoid of personal gesture and thus more 118 closely allied to Minimalist work of the period. Adolph Gottlieb worked in both lithography and silkscreen, but his characteristic theme of the period, two opposing forms, one above the other and generally calligraphic in form, called for a more creative use of the processes than he was willing to undertake. More successful, perhaps, than any other of the gestural painters who turned to printmaking in the 1960s was Helen Frankenthaler, whose unique contribution to painting was in the form of the stained canvas which she punctuated 119 with thin strokes of brilliant color. In her prints, mostly made at Universal Limited Art Editions, she has worked in lithography, etching, aquatint, and woodcut. She has created some of the most important prints in the mode of the action painters, notably because she has been able to translate into the print media the spirit of her style without trying to imitate the means she used to capture it on canvas.

Interest in collage or almost any manipulation of found objects was brought to an unusual degree of refinement during the 1950s in the

138

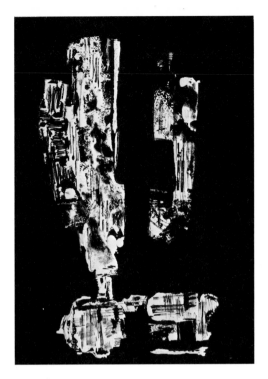

120 Louise Nevelson (b. 1900), Untitled, 1963. Lithograph, $31\frac{3}{8} \times 22$ (80 × 55·8). Gift of Kleiner, Bell and Co.

Surreal, magic boxes of Joseph Cornell and the wall sculptures of Louise Nevelson. Cornell, an eccentric recluse, made only three prints in all, and those in the year of his death, 1973. Nevelson made quite a few etchings in the New York Atelier 17 in the 1950s and many lithographs throughout the 1960s at Tamarind Lithography *120* Workshop in Los Angeles. They bear little resemblance to her monumental sculptures of stacked boxes containing dowels, balusters, and other manufactured wood shapes. Rather, the prints are filled with remarkably free, figurative and abstract jottings within confining lines or forms. Later Nevelson turned to embossed lead adhered to paper (the Italian Roberto Crippa used the technique in 1966) to produce images more closely resembling her sculptures.

In Europe after World War II the art situation was quite different from that in New York. The first decade found the center of the art world, Paris, more like a botanical garden in spring: the same plants with new flowers. However, artists whose work tended to be at cross-purposes with the French Cubist tradition before the war found after it that their more emotional approach to Abstraction had attracted an interested audience. Some of the younger traditional Abstractionists had exhibited their work during the war. Because their interpretations of the late styles of Klee and Kandinsky appeared to continue an acceptable form of art, they were appreciated even more. Both groups of abstract artists had the formidable and omnipresent example of several local old masters (Braque, Chagall, Léger, Matisse, and Picasso) with whom to compete for the growing audience for art. The printmaking projects of these older artists proliferated, and as facilities for printing were revived or established several of the younger artists began to devote a good part of their time to lithography and etching.

The prints of the younger traditionalists, such as Alfred Manessier, who followed the path of Roger Bissière, and Serge Poliakoff, were among the first color lithographs to show the tendency among post-war Abstractionists to create compositions with an overall rhythm of related forms that scattered the points of focus and demanded from the viewer attention to the entire picture plane. These and other artists working in this mode have produced many lithographs. One of the most talented of the painters who could have been characterized

as a true School of Paris Abstractionist was Nicolas de Staël. In his few prints – lithographs and woodcuts – he revealed a fresher, released character to the tiers of square and rectangular forms that populated his compositions. They were done during the last several years of his life when he used banner-bright colors in staccato rhythms. As with many of his landscape-related paintings, there is a strong horizontal flow to them.

121 Pierre Courtin (b. 1921), *Composition*, 1956. Engraving, $8\frac{13}{16} \times 9\frac{13}{16}$ (22·4 × 25). Gift of Theodore Schempp

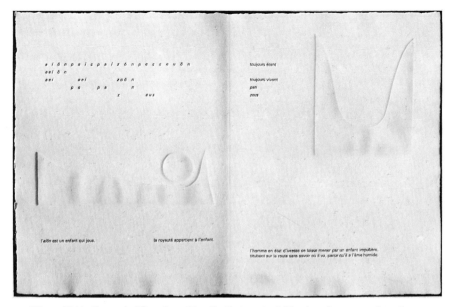

122 Etienne Hajdu (b. 1907), folio 9 from *Heraclite*. Paris, 1965. Inkless intaglio, page $17\frac{5}{8} \times 13\frac{7}{8}$ (44.7×35). Monroe Wheeler Fund

A similar propensity to build compositions from irregular blocks is also found in the engraved reliefs of Pierre Courtin. During the late 1950s he used jewelers' tools to transform his zinc plates into a sculptural relief which he then used to print, deeply embossing the thick paper and imparting a single earth tone overall. Because of the difficulty of retaining the shapes within the plate, which has to withstand extreme pressure during printing, Courtin's editions are small. *121*

It was inevitable that there would be sculptors who would work in a similar direction when it became possible for them to make prints. Henri-Georges Adam, the son of a goldsmith, created abstract etchings made of large cut-out plates filled with networks of lines. Etienne Hajdu utilized the deep embossing of intaglio, and his several books of embossed prints, done in collaboration with the designer and poet Pierre Lecuire, are examples of the degree of refinement that the French *livre du peintre* had attained. The brilliant conjunction of type and image that Bonnard and Vollard had achieved in 1900, and which subsequent artists and publishers had sought to emulate or improve, Hajdu extends through the use of embossing to create images on both sides of the page that simultaneously forecast and abstractly illustrate the text. *122*

141

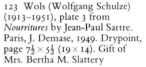

123 Wols (Wolfgang Schulze)
(1913–1951), plate 3 from
Nourritures by Jean-Paul Sartre.
Paris, J. Demase, 1949. Drypoint,
page $7\frac{1}{2} \times 5\frac{1}{2}$ (19 × 14). Gift of
Mrs. Bertha M. Slattery

The familial ties of these Parisian artists with the prewar Abstraction-Creation group (Arp and the Uruguayan Torres-Garcia most
notably) virtually erase World War II in the natural evolution of this
particular combination of influences. On the other hand, the war
engendered a higher tolerance for more Expressionist and forceful
presentation. Existentialism found its adherents among those young
enough to associate themselves directly with extreme change, old
enough to have been aware of the horror of the war years. The small
group that surrounded Jean-Paul Sartre in the early postwar years
transmitted in their own creations some of the same anguish that
emanated from the New York painters, Pollock in particular. The
work of Wols (Wolfgang Schulze) was the first of this genre to be
shown in postwar Paris. Under the constant influence of alcohol,
Wols composed unconsciously, revealing through his scratches and
barbed lines the abstract imagery of a tortured life. Sartre occasionally
123   supported him, and for Sartre's short story *Nourritures* (Paris, Jacques
Demase, 1949) Wols produced three drypoint illustrations. Most of
Wols's prints were made to illustrate books during the late 1940s, in
the traditional Parisian collaboration of the most progressive artists
and writers. 'L'art informel,' the name given to the abstract gestural
art of the European artists, encompassed artists like Wols, who had

142

not seriously painted before the war broke out, and Hans Hartung, who had been working in the Expressionist mode for decades.

Hartung's style of painting grew out of his tendency to do away with figurative elements in the models he chose to emulate: Nolde and Kokoschka in his youth, Julio Gonzalez just before World War II. It was during the period that he worked with Gonzalez that he made his first prints since his schooldays. At that moment his style of abstract improvisation took its unique direction, and after the war it gained strength and confidence. Hartung's vigorous strokes appear at first to be quite freely executed, but, unlike those of Wols or Pollock, they are the result of the same sort of refined calculation as the pitcher's curve ball in baseball. Hartung's forays into lithography and etching *124* have been frequent and intense. His first lithographs appeared in 1946. Hartung's final triumph occurred in 1960 with his acquisition of the Grand Prize of the Venice Biennale. That year, in which the public door to gestural painting was opened, also gave both European and American artists access to a larger audience through printmaking. Throughout the 1960s Hartung created lithographs in which his linear freedom increased in direct proportion to his ability to control each stroke. The tracks of his crayon or brush generally begin and

124 Hans Hartung (b. 1904), *Sheaf*, 1953. Etching and aquatint, $20\frac{5}{8} \times 15\frac{1}{4}$ (52·3 × 38·7). Larry Aldrich Fund

125 Pierre Soulages (b. 1919), *Composition IV*, 1957. Etching, $21\frac{5}{8} \times 15\frac{1}{4}$ (54·3 × 38·7). Gift of Mr. and Mrs. Armand P. Bartos

end within the rectangular barriers of the lithographic stone or etching plate, but when the outline is not included as part of the composition, the character of the space represented changes. The lines cross each other in a deep but undefined space and appear related to light shows and fireworks displays.

Caught more permanently on the picture plane even though no boundary restricts the eye are the etchings of Pierre Soulages. His large calligraphic signs are made up of wide sweeps of the brush, generally in vertical and horizontal directions. In order to capture the power and unity of this image in print, Soulages etches away the vacant portion of his plate so that the strokes, made by a scraper, alone remain. The single monumental sign emerged in Soulages's work in the mid-1950s, after a more linear period. Intense blacks that surround and are illuminated by nature's colors are the backbone of any Soulages composition. The appellation 'gestural art' does not completely describe Soulages's compositions, which are highly refined, stable structures.

The informality of the facture in this area of European art had many degrees of concept and interpretation. Soulages and Hartung created determined constructs of gestural line, while the Spaniard Antoni Tàpies conceived in his art a relationship between the uncontrollable traces of time and premeditated gestural lines, or graffiti. He began his career as a Surrealist painter, well aware of the heritage he shared with his fellow Catalan, Miró, but even more inclined to emulate the younger Parisian painters. Around 1954 he became deeply concerned with the physical remains of man's journey through his environment. He began painting these time-worn and defaced doors and walls, using sand and plaster to emulate the strata of their histories. He began to make lithographs in 1959, embossing them to obtain a similar tactile effect. Later he was to tear his prints and layer the printed sheets. More and more the element of graffiti encroaches upon the already brutalized surfaces, and while there are occasional recognizable letters and words, the lines cohere and, like true graffiti, entangle and depersonalize themselves. During the late 1960s Tàpies added etching to his repertoire, and during the student protests of 1968 he often depicted the walls of social struggle, covered with bloodied handprints and militant Xs. Most of Tàpies's prints have been published by Galerie Maeght in Paris or Sala Gaspar in Barcelona. There are often many points of similarity between Tàpies's spirited

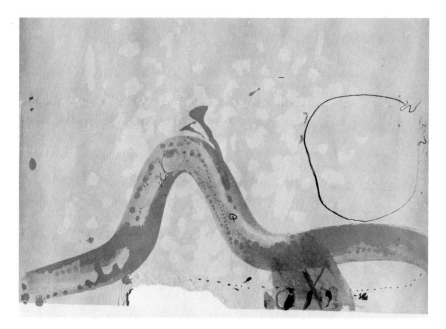

126 Antoni Tàpies Puig (b. 1923), *Number 15*, 1960. Lithograph, 20⅜ × 29 (51·7 × 73·6). Gift of Mr. and Mrs. Ralph F. Colin

evocations of decay and defacement and Miró's prints of the late 1960s, also issued by the same publishers. Tàpies has also illustrated many books, in which the prints are occasionally folded, torn, or collaged.

In other European countries there was a similar striking out into new modes of expression. Most prominent of the Italian artists whose propensities were toward the destruction of older formalisms was Lucio Fontana. His postwar work concerned itself with space; he created a spatial environment with light in 1948 and formed a group of artists who subscribed to the tenets of his *Manifiesto Blanco*, issued in Buenos Aires in 1946, 'Color, the element of space, sound, the element of time, and movement, which is extended in time and in space, are the fundamental forces of the new art, which embraces the four dimensions of existence-time-space.' Fontana began to puncture his canvases in 1948 and to slash them ten years later. The emblematic disposition of the holes within the rectangular monochromatic canvas or a confining irregular oval is related to the similarly mono-lithic sign of Soulages. The idea of creating an unknown area or space by opening up the picture plane was also taken up by Tàpies. However, the added element of a monochromatic plane disturbed so violently by the intrusion of holes is Fontana's own. It is, therefore, not surprising that there was little popular appeal to his work, and not until the 1960s was he commissioned to make prints. Fontana's spatial concepts transferred well into intaglio, where the deep etching technique had already attracted lesser talents. Rupturing paper during printing, however, was an undesirable and ultimately painful occurrence – something to be avoided at all costs. But Fontana required this taboo process, and among the few prints that he made which best represent his intentions are those that have been punctured in a definite and orderly pattern, each hole marked by the torn edges of paper forced beyond its possible elastic properties.

127

There were many artists in Europe who worked in a totally non-objective gestural manner, and most of them produced some prints. In Germany the most prominent of the free Abstractionist painters who also made prints has been Ernst Wilhelm Nay. In the late 1950s he began to make color aquatints in which puffs of diluted color crowd each other. More dynamic and in the path of Hartung is the work of another German who has worked in Paris, K. R. H. Sonderborg. His flashing etchings of the late 1950s consist of strong diagonals

127 Lucio Fontana (1899–1968), plate 5 from *Sei Acquaforti Originali*. Rome, Marlborough, 1964. Etching, $13\frac{3}{16} \times 16\frac{3}{4}$ (33·5 × 42·5). Abby Aldrich Rockefeller Fund

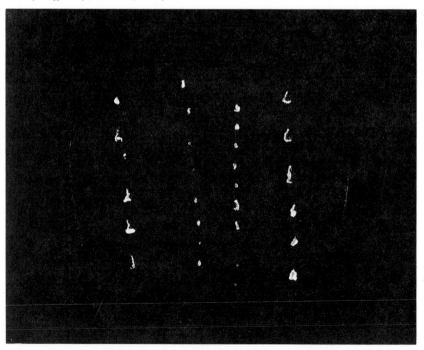

and arcs which seem to capture the essence of motion. Other Germans who began their work in printmaking in this area of abstraction include Fritz Winter and Hann Trier.

As recognition came to the abstract artist, publishers saw a rising demand for their prints, and painters who were so inclined began to meet that demand. Until the advent of Pop art, when graphic expression became an exceptionally large portion of artistic output, it was primarily the prints of European Abstractionists of both the above-noted tendencies that were available. The Italian painters Capogrossi, Severini, and Vedova, the Chinese Zao Wou-ki, the Dutch Bram van Velde, and the Belgian-born Gustave Singier all found their way to the lithographic studios during the 1950s. While their efforts have contributed little to the growth of the medium during a period when Braque, Miró, and Picasso were creating some of their best prints, they do represent the increasing awareness of the importance of prints as authentic and direct artistic expressions.

There were at the same time artists who introduced into their work recognizable imagery in a new form, divorced from Surrealism but sharing with it a dependence on psychological factors that contributed a disturbingly unstable effect. The postwar figurative artists in Europe were products of the war, and like the practitioners of l'art informel, they could no longer create peaceful compositions in which objectivity and formal analysis were the primary motivations.

In 1948 a group of artists from Scandinavia and the Lowlands joined together in Paris to form the group COBRA (the name composed from their capital cities, Copenhagen, Brussels, and Amsterdam). The eldest and most experienced of the group was the Danish artist Asger Jorn, but the Dutch artists Karel Appel, Cornelis Corneille, and George Constant were the nucleus of the Experimental Group from which COBRA grew. The Belgian Pierre Alechinsky became the youngest member when he joined his friend, the poet Christian Dotrement, who had acted as the catalyst in consolidating and forming COBRA.

COBRA as a common effort was short-lived (1948–51), but most of its members adhered to its Expressionist and mythological bases throughout their artistic careers. Taking the particular iconography of the folklore of their countries, they combined animate imagery with turbulent execution. The subject of their compositions, including the obvious representation of a cobra or snakelike creature, emulate

147

to some extent the terrifying possibilities of fairy tales. While Surrealists created pictures that alluded to complex and deep-seated fears, the COBRA artists put into their work the fascination of self-provoked fear. Goblins, creatures of strange, threatening shapes, and all manner of magical objects fill the works of Jorn and Appel.

Before his association with COBRA, Jorn had worked in Paris with Léger and Le Corbusier, conducted underground activities during the Nazi occupation of Denmark, and already had produced a considerable number of woodcuts, lithographs, and etchings. More than any of the others, Jorn was compelled to reveal in his work the dire effects of war consciousness. He was also suffering from tuberculosis during the COBRA period and in 1951 entered a sanatorium. Throughout his adult life he was a prolific writer and participated in many activities (including another short-lived art movement, the International Situationists, during 1957–61). His involvement with the Museum in Silkeborg, Denmark, established its prominent position in the exhibition of Wols, Michaux, and Dubuffet. In print-making Jorn was certainly the most dedicated among his temperamental colleagues in COBRA, who all made prints. During the early 1960s he and Appel created quantities of lithographs in which color surges across the page in broad swaths, occasionally massing to

128 Asger Jorn (1914–1973), *Masculine Resistance*, 1953. Etching, $4\frac{7}{8} \times 4\frac{5}{8}$ (12·4 × 11·7). Gift of Mr. and Mrs. Peter A. Rübel

129 (*right*) Pierre Alechinsky (b. 1927), pages 148–149 from *1¢ Life* by Walasse Ting. Berne, Kornfeld, 1964. Lithograph, $16\frac{1}{8} \times 23$ (40·9 × 58·4). Gift of Walasse Ting, Sam Francis and E. W. Kornfeld

divulge a wide-eyed monster. Appel later removed from his color patches the activating, Expressionist tracings which had bound his work to Jorn's, and created from these unmodulated and brilliant color masses a race of carnival creatures.

Adhering more to Jorn's linear, emotion-driven composition, Pierre Alechinsky has probably been more directly concerned with printmaking than any of the COBRAs except Jorn. After the movement was disbanded, Alechinsky began to work in Hayter's re-established Atelier 17 in Paris. Alechinsky often collaborated with his friend Dotrement, combining verse and illustration in the same print (they contributed an etching to the portfolio *21 Etchings and Poems*, mentioned earlier). Oriental calligraphy influenced Alechinsky's execution, and his forms emerge from complex tangles of line. During the 1960s he worked on several projects with the Chinese poet-painter Walasse Ting. With Sam Francis, whose work was also partly activated by Oriental methods, Ting created the foremost illustrated book of the early 1960s, *1¢ Life* (Berne, Kornfeld, 1964), 129 for which Alechinsky, Jorn, and Appel created several color lithographs. The volume provides the sole example of the conjunction of European and American gestural art and its American successor, Pop art.

The most important figurative artist to emerge directly after the war was Jean Dubuffet. The former wine merchant who had left his artistic aspirations behind in the early 1920s turned again to art when the war made commerce difficult, if not impossible. His first exhibition came in 1944, the same year he created his first book of lithographs *Matière et Memoire* (Paris, F. Mourlot, 1945). His intense interest in the art of the insane, children, and primitive peoples was the basis for his formulation of an expressive style. Unlike his friend Jorn, who struggled with contemporary social concerns, Dubuffet preferred to depict the most ordinary and timeless situations of life: birth, eating, being oneself (portraiture), and so on. Throughout the decade and a half after the war Dubuffet created a great number of prints, mainly lithographs, which were often grouped together in albums for which he occasionally provided text. He was, for a time, fascinated with natural materials, which he would use to create paintings, sculpture, and collages as well as to transfer their images and make drawings and lithographs from these imprints. From leaves, stones, dirt, and other unlikely found matter, Dubuffet created compositions populated by grotesque human and animal figures in imaginary settings. The fairy-tale aspect of postwar figurative Expressionism is most comfortable in Dubuffet's creations. *Work and Play* (1953) is typical of the imprint lithographs in which figurative elements have been found and outlined in a relatively chance-produced composition. The three floating figures have neither contact nor any definable relationship to each other. There are elements of humor and fear in Dubuffet's work which he offers in the most ingenuous manner by means of extreme simplification of execution and content.

Dubuffet's romance with lithography in the late 1950s is one of the important milestones in the history of the dedication painters have shown to printmaking in the twentieth century. Exploring the infinite possibilities of producing texture on a lithographic stone or plate, Dubuffet transferred natural materials of every kind to the stone as well as placing liquids of several sorts on their surfaces, blotting, or burning them. Two hundred and thirty-four black and white lithographs emerged as a basic set for further experimentation. These prints made up the first thirteen of the albums generally titled *Phenomena* (1959). Certain lithographs of this artist's palette of textures were combined and printed in color, sometimes as many as ten

130

130 Jean Dubuffet (1901–1985),
Work and Play, 1953. Lithograph,
$25\frac{3}{4} \times 19\frac{13}{16}$ (65·4 × 50·3). Gift of
Mr. and Mrs. Ralph F. Colin

for a single print. Serge Lozingot was the master printer who worked on Dubuffet's own press to accomplish the *Phenomena* prints, as well as additional color trial proofs using the key *Phenomena* plates. The latter, with the key black and white prints and published color prints, brought the total of possible textures and color combinations that the artist was ultimately to use for his future compositions up to nearly two thousand.

A group of figurative lithographs was created out of the *Phenomena* project. For each of these color prints Dubuffet made a collage of cut-out trial proofs, added linear elements in ink on acetate and translucent whites with cut-out drafting paper. The finished maquette was given to Lozingot to use as a guide for making the lithograph from the *Phenomena* plates that combined to make up the various color trial proofs. This complex and technically exhausting method was used to create portraits and scenes of a fresh, childlike nature.

147

Dubuffet's work of the 1960s continued to examine people, objects, and structures in a naïve, slightly insane, or primitive fashion. The 'Hourloupe' (a word created by Dubuffet) paintings, sculpture, and prints consist of extended networks of lines which join to form the outlines of the subject. In the early 1960s the lines were predominantly red and blue on a white ground. Grays and blacks were added, and the holes of the network were occasionally filled in to show depth. In the 1970s many works were simply black and white sculpture made of epoxy. Prints made during this period were chiefly silkscreens in the limited bright, flat colors of the 'Hourloupe' style, often grouped together in books or printed on plastic (vacuum-formed or contoured panels) as objects produced in editions ('multiples').

Few of the major postwar European painters of the figurative Expressionist persuasion have neglected the area of printmaking. The most notable exception has been Francis Bacon, the British artist whose writhing, screaming figures personify the trauma of a generation caught in an irremediable destiny. There were others, however, who manifested in their prints the helpless, threatened state of life in the post-atomic age. While not in conscious reaction to the world situation, the late, postwar work of Alberto Giacometti encompasses this condition. The drawn lithographs and etchings of Giacometti show his style of paring down the human form to its essential structure, its inner being or, more mystically, its soul. Quite unprotected by the controlled mask of experience, Giacometti's faces reveal the reality within. In the mid-1940s the meaning of what he was sculpting dawned upon him, 'This was no longer a living head but a thing I looked at like any other thing . . . like something that was alive as well as dead. I uttered a cry of terror. . . .'[29]

In Great Britain two artists of Giacometti's generation, Henry Moore and Graham Sutherland, had spent the early 1940s as official war artists, documenting the Battle of Britain and its effect on its people. They were both committed to Surrealism as the basis of their imagery, but after their experiences in the war years, it was inevitable that the frustratingly immutable nature of reality be expressed through a more emotionally driven line and choice of subject. Moore's earliest work in printmaking was an extension of his drawing during the war. His first group of lithographs were illustrations to Goethe's text of the Prometheus legend, translated by André Gide (*Prométhée*, Paris, Jonquières et Nicaise, 1951). The plates, which were made from

131

131 Alberto Giacometti (1901–1966), *Bust*, 1952. Lithograph, 14⅝ × 20⅝ (48·7 × 52·3).
Larry Aldrich Fund

drawings on acetate, show figures constructed of fragmented stone
moving through an undefined space. Moore, like Giacometti, had
no real commitment to the art of printmaking, so there is little continuity in his prints to divulge the progress of his vision as it relieved
itself of the memories of conflict. At the age of seventy-one Moore
created etchings for an album entitled *Elephant Skull* (Geneva,   *132*
Cramer, 1970) which return to the mystery of form itself without
evoking any sensation of the provocative nature of the beast from
which the form is derived.

Sutherland, who had made etchings in a conservative manner
during the 1920s, divided his time after the war between portraiture
and the depiction of natural objects in the Surrealist's indefinite space.
Neutral relationships between plants and animals in Sutherland's
compositions are compromised by their threatening forms. Thorns,
night creatures and other mysterious and menacing living things   *133*

153

were brought together in several color lithographs published in the 1950s. In color and freely brushed contours Sutherland exhibited an indebtedness to the German Expressionists, particularly Nolde. His most extensive work in printmaking was a *Bestiary* (1968) consisting of twenty-five color lithographs of insects, reptiles, birds, and animals.

A true heir of the German Expressionist tradition which was intrinsically printerly, Rolf Nesch had received his inspiration during a six-week visit with Kirchner. Nesch's first important prints were views of the bridges of Hamburg (1932) printed from collages of industrial metal materials (screening, die-stamped metal, and so forth). The Hamburg Sezession, to which he belonged, was dissolved in 1933, and Nesch moved to Norway. There he continued to work, coming under the spell of Munch and the awesome appearance of the northern landscape. His plates became increasingly complex, and as he could not vary their size on his own small press, he combined several prints into the larger format of triptychs and polyptychs. *The Herring Catch* (1938), the first of these, contains six panels. Nesch made further use of his plates and their various elements in metal reliefs, and increasingly his entire work evolved from his unique printing medium.

Nesch's imagery became more dreamlike after a serious accident he suffered during World War II. Additional figurative elements appeared in which wit, humor, and terror were combined. Nesch's postwar work was widely exhibited in the 1950s and was one of the influences that brought a strong emphasis on material and technique into the field of printmaking. The assemblage of junk, particularly machine-made materials, became a major artistic concern after World War II, and Nesch's early explorations in this area, on a purely emotional rather than rational basis, were prophetic.

Other artists who have worked in the Expressionist figurative style and produced prints that successfully recapitulated their painterly concerns are the Spaniard Antonio Saura, the Polish-born Maryan, the Mexican Rufino Tamayo, and the Americans Leon Golub and Jack Levine. Some sculptors, too, such as the late Reg Butler, Marino Marini, and Jacques Lipchitz, augmented their postwar creative efforts with a few prints. It was left to younger artists who had grown to adulthood during the war to reveal through their choices of imagery and execution the paralysis of spirit that arose from that disaster. Like those of Bacon, Giacometti, and Sutherland, their

132 *(right)* Henry Moore (1898–1986), plate 10 from *Elephant Skull*. Geneva, Cramer, 1970. Etching, $11\frac{9}{16} \times 7\frac{13}{16}$ (29·4 × 19·8). Gift of the artist and Galerie Gerald Cramer

133 *(below)* Graham Sutherland (1903–1980), *Crown of Thorns*, 1955. Lithograph, $18\frac{1}{2} \times 25\frac{1}{2}$ (47 × 64·7). Purchase

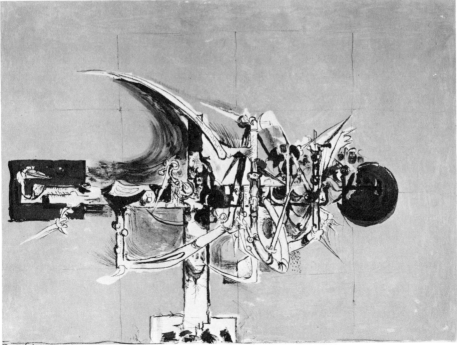

compositions were most often amalgams of Surrealist form and Expressionist execution. To this, many added a particularly eccentric vocabulary acquired for the most part from mystically oriented art of the past.

The most extreme examples of this synthesis developed in Vienna, where Ernst Fuchs and Friedrich Hundertwasser (Friedrich Stowasser) represented the two poles of fantastic art as it wavered between the Surreal and the Expressionist. Both artists could be classified as obsessed, Fuchs with religious mysticism, Hundertwasser with his environment. Fuchs has emulated an obsessed artist of another place and century, William Blake, in his skillful and tireless dedication to etching. Technically, Fuchs has no peer in the compulsively precise execution of his plates. While his subjects are nearly always without contemporary motifs, they have a symbolic relevance to contemporary conditions. Fuchs consistently turns to ancient religious (Christian, Hindu, and other) representation for his forms, while Hundertwasser is influenced by the decorative effects obtained by Klimt and other Jugendstil artists at the turn of the century. He has extended their spiraling motifs, turning them into convulsive environments in which brilliant colors add to the effect of hysteria. Hundertwasser's prints, generally color lithographs and silkscreens, recapitulate the subjects of his paintings. Several silkscreens have been published in extremely large editions (ten thousand) in an effort to distribute his images

135

151

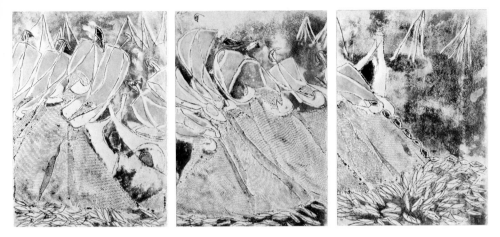

134 Rolf Nesch (1893–1975), *The Herring Catch*, 1938. Metal print in 6 panels, each plate 23⅝ × 16½ (60 × 42). Gift of Mr. and Mrs. Alfred Jaretzki, Jr.

widely and directly combat the commercial emphasis on limitation. He has endeavored, through his art as well as in his lifestyle, to fight functionalism and other signs of depersonalization.

It was this concern about the future of humanity, shared by many younger postwar artists during the 1950s, that compelled them to become increasingly concerned with man's image. The work of three Germans, Horst Antes, Horst Janssen, and Paul Wunderlich, all of whom spent their youth under the swastika banner of the Nazis, represents this direction in a way quite different from that expressed in Germany after World War I. Rather than depict man's conscious transgressions, they placed man at the mercy of his subconscious or elemental drives. Years of Surrealist philosophy and Freudian psychology influenced these three artists who matured in an occupied land that allowed them every creative opportunity but constantly teased them with their communal guilt.

The eldest, Paul Wunderlich, derived his figurative style from biological charts, and his early subjects were often renderings of the physical details of human beings metamorphosed into fantastic creatures. He began his artistic career as a lithographer, studying at the Landeskunstschule in Hamburg, and printed more than one hundred of his own editions. His technique, particularly using *tusche* – the greasy ink used in drawing on the stone – is impressive and enlivens each image. Wunderlich inserts into almost all his work an

157

135 Ernst Fuchs (b. 1930), *St. George*, 1958. Etching, $9\frac{1}{2} \times 6\frac{7}{16}$ ($24 \times 16\cdot3$). Lent anonymously

136 aura of spatial or subject disorientation. He will duplicate his main subject, reversing the second image or placing it above or below the first. While many of his compositions of the 1950s and early 1960s were explicitly provocative, either because of their Surreal depiction of sexual acts or their political antagonism, Wunderlich increasingly found the decadent curves of Art Nouveau expressive of postwar opulence. His subsequent prints and paintings are filled with languid females lying on zebra skins or leaning on cabriole-legged chairs, in mauve and other smoke-obscured tones.

Horst Janssen, also from Hamburg, studied there and afterward opened a drinking club. His earliest etchings were done in 1957, and some of them parody Rembrandt paintings by distorting the respectable burghers of Rotterdam into insect-like beings. He shares with Klee and Ensor a sardonic streak of humor that is always more than cynicism. In his landscapes there is a portent of disaster among the broken branches and jagged hills. However, in the way of his generation, he is preoccupied with man, and, in his case, with himself, as the repository of society's ills. His self-portraits and the decomposing heads he etched for *Hannos Tod* (Rome, Pantheon, 1973) sum up in expressive form this artist's search for humanity.

The helmet-headed homunculus that Horst Antes created to be the vessel of his appraisal of mankind's aimless journey through life has undergone several transformations since it first appeared in his paintings and prints in the early 1960s. At first, influenced by the COBRA artists, the figure merged with gestural traces that made up its environment. Progressively, the figure was moved away from its surroundings and became either made up of the selected subject-matter (flags, roosters, and other popular devices) or moved through a completely hostile environment filled with more or less symbolic objects. The figure itself often has displayed stigmata or other references to suffering. Antes's prints in both etching and lithography display this archetypal human being as a timeless sign in contrast to the contemporaneous imagery of the Pop artist.

Naturally, the Expressionist influence was felt wherever European and American art was exhibited or reproduced. The paintings of

136 Paul Wunderlich (b. 1927), *Rendez-vous Technic II*, 1962. Lithograph, $24\frac{1}{16} \times 15\frac{9}{16}$ ($61 \times 39 \cdot 5$). Gift of Mr. and Mrs. Peter A. Rübel

137 Horst Janssen (b. 1929), *Melancholy Self Portrait*, 1965. Etching, $19 \times 15\frac{1}{2}$ ($48 \times 39 \cdot 3$). Mr. and Mrs. Peter A. Rübel Fund

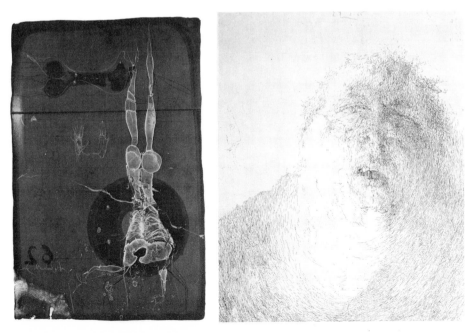

women by Willem de Kooning directly affected the Japanese print-maker Masuo Ikeda, one of whose prints includes the names of other artists he felt contributed to his formation: Wols, Klee, Giacometti, Dubuffet, and Pollock. Ikeda modified his early gestural style into a stylized figurative form, the Oriental equivalent in some ways to what Antes was doing. He, too, found Surrealism and the spatial mystery of Magritte, in particular, an important addition to his composition. Since his visits to Europe and the U.S.A. in the mid-1960s he has used his superb technique, mainly drypoint and mezzotint, to create prints depicting women in Surreal settings dominated by cubes of sky.

One postwar figurative artist, the Italian Enrico Baj, ambiguously performs somewhere in the area between Expressionist satire and playtime Dada. His portraits of generals and other personifications of authority are obfuscated with nonsensical or kitsch embellishments. Color is an important element in the rendering of Baj's carnival figures (they often resemble the stuffed dolls used as targets in ball-throwing games of skill), and during the 1960s a considerable number of his lithographs and aquatints in brilliant tones found a receptive audience. Unlike American Pop art, which also had powerful Dada antecedents, Baj's work appears to involve itself almost exclusively with satire aimed at the establishment. Relief prints of the same period by the Argentine Antonio Berni have similar subjects, while the Mexi-

138 Horst Antes (b. 1936), *Figure with Red P-Hat with Flag*, 1967. Lithograph, $21\frac{7}{8} \times 16\frac{5}{8}$ (55·5 × 42·2). Mrs. John D. Rockefeller 3rd Fund

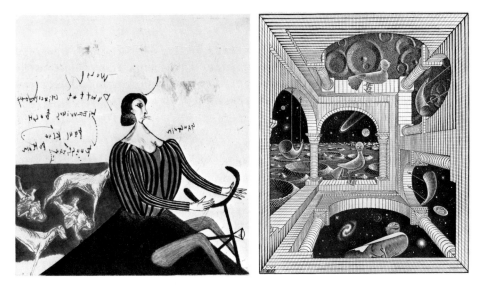

139 Masuo Ikeda (b. 1934), *Romantic Scene*, 1965. Drypoint, roulette and etching, $14\frac{5}{16} \times 13\frac{1}{4}$ ($36 \cdot 3 \times 33 \cdot 6$). Gift of the Felix and Helen Juda Foundation

140 M. C. Escher (1898–1972), *Other World*, 1947. Wood engraving, $12\frac{7}{16} \times 10\frac{1}{4}$ ($31 \cdot 6 \times 26$). Purchase Fund

can José Luis Cuevas utilizes in his lithographs, as does Baj, many literary references of a very personal, jaundiced view of society.

There are two printmakers of the postwar period whose imagery gives the impression of Surrealist influence but who are, rather, unique stylists of inimitable technical facility. Yozo Hamaguchi, a Japanese who settled in Paris after the war (he had been a student there during the 1930s), is the master of mezzotint. His mysterious still lifes, in which a single walnut or bunch of asparagus, placed in a limitless *141* setting, activates the total picture plane, capture the precious quality of a Japanese household ceremony in finite form. The velvety surface of Hamaguchi's mezzotints is endlessly seductive, and the minimal subject-matter in such a form has appealed to those who search for that illusory perfection worthy of spiritual meditation.

Maurits Cornelius Escher, a Dutch printmaker who lived mainly in Italy before the war, developed into a master craftsman very early in his career. His ability to cut and engrave wood precisely was an important adjunct to his obsessive attempt to confront 'the enigmas that surround us', bringing him into 'the domain of mathematics.'[30] Escher's work generally concerns distortion, sometimes through breaking up the picture plane into regular, infinitely repetitive

161

patterns, through metamorphosis by the interaction of repetitive forms, by means of fraction through the imposition of geometric figures, and through simultaneous representation of conflicting spatial concepts. This latter means is seen in his wood-engraving *Other World* (1947), in which an impossible triple view of architectural and astronomical space is populated by three human-headed birds. During the 1960s young people looking for 'mind-expanding' experiences through the use of LSD found that Escher's images complemented the visions they had during their drugged periods. The precision of his line, the simultaneity of different perspectives, and the extended pattern-making and distortion put Escher's work at the unusual juncture where the opposed sensitivities of scientist and mentally disturbed meet.

The art of the mentally disturbed was of particular interest to Dubuffet, as we have seen. One cannot honestly categorize Escher's visionary prints as the result of mental aberration, but an obsessive interest in schematism does have a different interpretation when applied to the prints of another Dutch printmaker, Anton Heyboer. Born in Indonesia and having led a peripatetic childhood, Heyboer was left for dead in a Nazi work camp when he was nineteen. He made his

140

141 Yozo Hamaguchi (b. 1909), *Asparagus and Lemon*, 1957. Mezzotint, $11\frac{3}{4} \times 17\frac{1}{2}$ (29·8 × 44·5). Gift of Heinz Berggruen

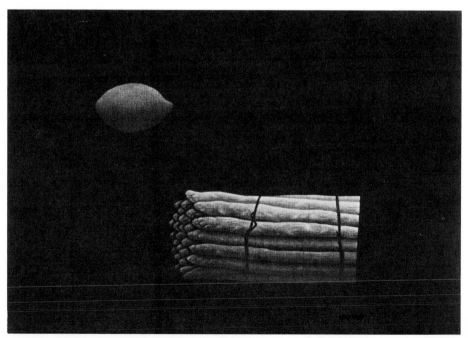

142 Anton Heyboer (b. 1924), *The System with Figure*, 1957. Etching, $8\frac{3}{16} \times 10\frac{3}{4}$ (20·8 × 27·3). Gift of Mr. and Mrs. Armand P. Bartos

first etchings after he had been confined in a mental sanatorium in 1951. His subsequent experiences with the Amsterdam artists' circle in the mid-1950s, alcoholism, and broken marriages determined for him the form and content of his artistic expression. Heyboer's unusual *142* etchings are diagrams that simultaneously put his warped life experiences in a systematic order and solve daily problems for him and his household. The plates, made of roofing zinc, are etched in a primitive manner and are covered with statements, numbered diagrams, and occasional stylized human figures. The plates are often printed by Heyboer's wife or companion in earth tones in the hut they occupy in the northern Dutch marshes.

During the 1950s younger artists were given the means to achieve some public recognition through the institution of international prizes and exhibitions. One of the earliest exhibitions to recognize the artistic value of prints was the International Biennial of Graphics in Ljubljana, Yugoslavia. By 1955, the year Ljubljana's competition was inaugurated, communications among countries had been considerably improved. There is no question that many of the international print exhibitions were established for political and economic gain. Yugoslavia independently straddled the Eastern European nations dominated by the Soviet Union and the Western nations with which it was eager to promote trade and tourism. Having found that art was an exportable commodity, the government of Yugoslavia sanctioned the Ljubljana exhibition with the intention of not only showing the work of its own artists but bringing to them the best examples of printmaking from all over the world. The variety in concept and quality with which the Yugoslav artists were bombarded has led to their development as international artists.

Of course, there were many other countries with similar goals, whether fundamentally cultural, political, or economic, and large international biennial exhibitions of prints have taken place for over a decade in Tokyo, Grenchen, and Lugano, and for a shorter period in Krakow, Florence, and Bradford. Regional (by continent or groups of countries) competitions have also proliferated, particularly in Latin America. The most important prizes for prints during this twenty-year period were given, however, at the large multi-media biennials in Venice and São Paulo. Miró was the winner in Venice in 1954 and not in Ljubljana until 1965. Few unestablished artists have gained the first or grand awards. Local artists won more important prizes as their biennials aged, and the organizers have tended to promote their nation's artists in each other's biennials. Among the talented Yugoslavs and Japanese who have triumphed in the two most important biennials are Janez Bernik, Riko Debenjak, Andrej Jemec, Miroslav Sutej, Tetsuya Noda, Kosuke Kimura, and Jiro Takamatsu. Regrettably, the roster of biennial prizewinners seems to be less a record of lasting contributions to the art of the print than a somewhat limited chronicle of the taste of the period.

10 The flourishing of lithography in the U.S.A.: the prints of Pop art

IN THE LATE 1950s excellent conditions for the widespread acceptance of American artists existed. In addition, a small part of the more culturally aware and affluent American public, which had already patronized the lithographs and etchings of Chagall and Picasso, seemed prepared to support the market for its own contemporary art. Several astute persons who were enthusiastic about the new importance of American art saw that the time was ripe for these painters and sculptors to make prints. Calling upon the American foundation system, which provided great quantities of money for social and cultural purposes, June Wayne established Tamarind Lithography Workshop in Los Angeles in 1960. June Wayne's experiences as an artist in search of a place to make prints had brought her to the conclusion that the U.S.A. needed not only one shop such as Mourlot's, but several. She received a grant from the Ford Foundation to set up a workshop where experienced lithography printers would work with students, already trained in an art school or university, in a master-and-apprentice system. The students would progress as they mastered successively more complex techniques until they became master lithographers, at which time they either succeeded the shop master, set up their own shops, or became teachers of lithography.

The program that made Tamarind more than a school for lithographers, however, was the introduction of practicing artists to lithography. Coincidentally, as the artists used the workshop facility, they provided the problems and work for the students. This essential interdependence was a positive benefit to the students, for it taught them some of the psychology necessary in working well with artists. Such a creative collaboration was fairly simple to achieve at Tamarind since most of the students had, unlike commercial printers, started as art students. For most of the 104 artists who came to Tamarind during the decade of its existence, their two-month fellowships at Tamarind Workshop introduced them to a new medium. The program drew them away from the solitude of their studios and into a more structured work situation which, for many, did not allow the latitude of time, space, and contemplation for the development of masterpieces. Those artists who were already familiar with lithography were better able to accomplish what they planned at Tamarind, though they were often hampered by the necessity of working with student printers who were not experienced enough to give technical advice. What basically shaped most Tamarind-printed lithographs, however, was the fact that the artist was encouraged to continue producing rather than subject each work to his own critical evaluation over a period of time. This mode of working was the reverse of what had become habitual to American artists. The stringent rules of European academies, which fostered the concept that artists be prepared to produce on demand, were unknown in American fine-art schools, though this attitude prevailed in commercial-art schools. The efficient production of advertising art was only slightly compromised by artists who were considered very creative and thus liable to some deviation from the rules. Even so, a successful commercial artist like Andy Warhol was expected to produce on demand, and did. Thus, at Tamarind, it was the artists who were commercially trained or already acquainted with the workshop situation who created the best prints. Among the latter were Sam Francis and Louise Nevelson. As the second or California wave of Pop artists appeared (and although they only occasionally shared Warhol's commercial background, they were committed to the more rigid production methods of modern technology), some of them, such as Ed Ruscha and Billy Al Bengston, were successful at Tamarind. The ultimate value of the Tamarind experiment was in the proliferation of lithographic shops it fostered in North America. By the mid-1960s there were several in California, and Tamarind printers were staffing new shops in the Midwest and on the East Coast.

At almost the same moment that Tamarind was established, Mrs. Tatyana Grosman, in her home outside New York City, was taking an altogether different approach to lithography. Her Universal Limited Art Editions succeeded her husband's efforts to supplement their income from his painting by producing serigraph reproductions. After he became ill, Mrs. Grosman was encouraged by the American sculptress Mary Callery in her desire to provide a place for artists to make lithographs. Mrs. Grosman offered her lithograph press at first to two friends, Larry Rivers and Fritz Glarner. In 1960 she invited a younger painter, Jasper Johns, to her shop, and in 1962 Robert Rauschenberg began to work there. The lithographs they made at Universal were to fully demonstrate for the first time in prints the vitality of the new American art. By 1963 Rauschenberg was able to create a print, *Accident*, that was to win the First Prize at the Fifth International Biennial of Graphics in Ljubljana, a year before he was recognized as worthy of the Grand Prize at the Venice Biennale.

While printmaking played a seminal role in the development of the painter Jackson Pollock, this art form was never a major concern of the Abstract Expressionists. It took the active encouragement of Mrs. Grosman, her long experience of the work patterns of the New York School of painters, her incredible patience and determination that only the best of an artist's work be published, to enable artists to produce prints equal in quality to their paintings. One other substantial contribution made by Mrs. Grosman to the art of printmaking was her feeling for the materials of her craft. She recognized that artists who chose materials for assemblages and took such an interest in the craft of creating art would demand equal care in the choice of materials for their prints. She commissioned handmade papers and continually offered choices through which the artist could extend and refine his concept. While there were cases where this search for perfection led to annoying delays, collaboration was always seen as more important than compromise. The physical limitations of the Grosmans' shop (which was set up in the garage of their home) necessitated the restriction to invited artists only. In addition, Mrs. Grosman felt that working with artists with whom she had little or no *rapport* would be unproductive. The American artists who made lithographs at Universal during the 1960s were Lee Bontecou, Jim Dine, Helen Frankenthaler, Fritz Glarner, Robert Goodnough, Grace Hartigan, Jasper Johns, Robert Motherwell, Robert Rauschenberg, Larry Rivers, and James Rosenquist. The Venezuelan sculptor who was part of the New York Pop movement, Marisol, also worked at Universal. With the exception of Goodnough and Hartigan, these artists continued to create prints at Universal over many years, and most into the 1970s.

The Tamarind and Universal workshops provided the technological possibilities for the production of prints. They served some artists who had already presented in their paintings and sculptures the essentials of a new visual experience which found form under two historical influences: the part of Surrealism that had engendered Abstract Expressionism and Dada. The freedom of action painting emphasized the surface of the pigment applied through dripping or swabbing with large brushes. A fresh feeling for the materials of painting evolved and opened the way for further experimentation with other materials, such as newspapers, photographs and, ultimately, trash. The assemblage of discarded objects was a connection that an artist like Robert Rauschenberg had with the German exponent of Dada, Kurt Schwitters. Schwitters organized his collage compositions by adding forms or areas of solid color; Rauschenberg drew his photoimages together with vigorous brush work. Both sought to disrupt the equilibrium of the spectator by preventing a systematic reading of the pictorial or lettered elements through the disturbance of disparate subjects or concealed forms. As Rauschenberg worked away from the Abstract Expressionist formulae, he concentrated more upon found objects, the photographic images he selected from magazines predominating in his prints. While the images he chose often focused on a particular subject, they were rarely combined in a narrative fashion. His compositions were stroboscopically choreographed so that the portions of representative material would be sensed in the same manner as the eye senses the total environment. Rauschenberg allows the viewer the same visual choices that are made in life, away from art, in which accumulations of miscellaneous, disparate materials are taken in by the eye on the basis of form, then ordered by the mind into learned sequences. It is the latter stage that Rauschenberg sabotages by eliminating conjunctive pictorial elements that would allow the photoimages or accumulations of trash to make sense.

144   The lithograph *Accident* of 1963 is typical of the transition that marked the end of purely action art. Almost the entire composition is filled with broad brush work, nearly concealing the photographic plates that were later to dominate in Rauschenberg's prints. The large lithographic stone broke during proofing, and this unexpected event added a dynamic diagonal element to the composition which, in terms of Abstract Expressionism, would have been characterized as fortuitous. Beyond welcoming that diagonal, however, Rauschenberg decided to retain the bits of broken stone by incorporating them into what had been the lower margin – thus asserting that the process

143 Sam Francis (b. 1923), *The White Line*, 1960. Lithograph, $35\frac{11}{16} \times 24\frac{7}{8}$ (90·6 × 63). Gift of E. W. Kornfeld

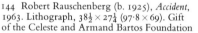

144 Robert Rauschenberg (b. 1925), *Accident*, 1963. Lithograph, $38\frac{1}{2} \times 27\frac{1}{4}$ (97·8 × 69). Gift of the Celeste and Armand Bartos Foundation

by which art is created is important in itself. Process would become a major characteristic of the next decade's art, with the use of silkscreen and photographic manipulation dominating and redefining the fields of painting and printmaking.

The problematic decision to return to the object by artists weaned on totally abstract art is dealt with best in the work of Jasper Johns. While he retained a persuasive personal application in creating the surface of his paintings and prints, technique was at the service of a diametrically opposed concept: rather than take as his subject the revelation of an object through the interpretation of a series of abstract markings, Johns chose to take an object which was superficially an abstract two-dimensional pattern. While his choice to use the series of concentric circles of a target alone did not reveal an altogether new direction, the selection of the American flag added an emotionally charged dimension to what was essentially an artist's determination to maintain the stability of a two-dimensional surface. The lithograph *Flag I* was one of Johns's earliest prints, done at Universal Limited Art

145

Editions in 1960. This print, like the paintings that preceded it in the late 1950s, was one of the first to promulgate the newly ambiguous aspect of the object in art. The earlier abstract art of the 1930s had only occasionally incorporated objects of the contemporary environment and then exclusively as part of a composition. By contrast, Johns used an object so totally integrated into his own culture that it was simultaneously too familiar to be visualized as art and too representative of a highly emotional patriotic fervor to be treated as nothing more than its physical entity. While Johns's purpose was to subject the object to the rule of the medium, inevitably the treatment of the medium itself changed. He has consistently formed his work on the basis of superb draftsmanship and consummate work with brush and palette knife. Within these broadly classical limitations Johns has created works of unique quality. His most compelling lithograph was *Ale Cans*, of 1964, in which he portrayed his sculpture of two Ballantine ale cans, a painted bronze piece in which one of the cans appears to be punctured. The sculpture, as is to be expected, was *after* the beer cans, not *of* them (that is, not cast from original cans), and was meant to induce the enigma of reality confused with art by the introduction of a realistic situation (the can opened for drinking) in a facsimile object. Going one step further, and also commenting on the function of prints carrying information, Johns created a portrait of his sculpture in lithography, carefully drawing it on the stone in perspective and just as carefully removing the enclosing space that surrounded it and defining the true two-dimensionality of his picture by framing the blackened background with crayon lines.

145 Jasper Johns
(b. 1930), *Flag I*, 1960.
Lithograph, $17\frac{1}{2} \times 26\frac{3}{4}$
($44 \cdot 5 \times 68$). Gift of
Mr. and Mrs.
Armand P. Bartos

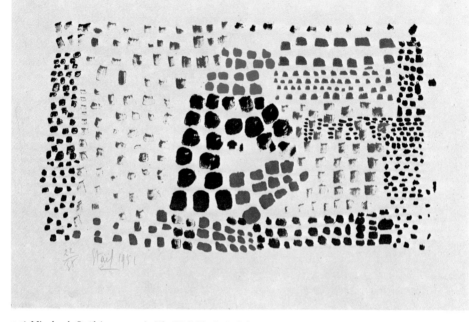

146 Nicolas de Staël (1914–1955), *The Wall (Study in Color No. I)*, 1951. Lithograph, sheet $19\frac{7}{8} \times 25\frac{3}{4}$ (50·5 × 65·4). Abby Aldrich Rockefeller Fund

Johns continued to make lithographs throughout the 1960s and into the 1970s both at Universal and at Gemini G.E.L., a shop in Los Angeles opened by a former Tamarind printer, Ken Tyler. Tyler was enthusiastic about the prospects of expanding the medium of lithography by encouraging the foremost American artists to work freely at his shop. He created new machinery and brought the known techniques to a high degree of efficiency, thus inducing artists to give free rein to their demands for new and better ways of achieving their concepts. For Johns, Gemini developed a means of producing a spectrum (or rainbow) effect over a large surface (the series *Colored Numerals* of 1969). For Rauschenberg, who was then creating compositions almost exclusively from newspaper and magazine photographs, Tyler produced the largest lithograph ever made, *Sky Garden* (1969). Both artists continue to explore the infinite possibilities of the print media: Johns has worked in an altogether fresh manner on lithographic plates printed on an offset press; Rauschenberg has combined the art of

147 Jean Dubuffet (1901–1985), *Carrot Nose*, 1962. Lithograph, $23\frac{13}{16} \times 14\frac{7}{8}$ (60·5 × 37·7). Gift of Mr. and Mrs. Ralph F. Colin

making prints with that of making paper, thereby creating a totally new artistic unity of two ancient crafts. However exploratory and imaginative their approach to printmaking has been, the value of Johns's and Rauschenberg's work rests on the imagery with which they turned around a two-decade habit of dependence on nonobjective art. Whereas the main swing in painting during the 1940s and 1950s was away from the object, much of the art of the 1960s evolved from a nearly desperate search for the most banal and unseemly objects in a posttechnological environment.

Emerging at the same moment as Rauschenberg and Johns were two American artists who continued to emphasize the romantic and subjective in their works. Like their contemporaries, both Larry Rivers and Jim Dine had a strong attachment to the physical activity of painting. They, too, surrounded or embellished the real objects they selected with sweeping brush strokes and drips of paint. Rivers, essentially a figurative painter tied to the same tradition, one might say, that made de Kooning return to painting women in the early 1950s, dwelt on the human aspects of his subjects. His paintings and

148 Larry Rivers (b. 1923), *Lucky Strike in the Mirror II*, 1960–63. Lithograph, $26\frac{1}{4} \times 18\frac{1}{4}$ (66·6 × 46·3). Gift of the Celeste and Armand Bartos Foundation

149 Jim Dine (b. 1935), *Eleven Part Self Portrait (Red Pony)*, 1965. Lithograph, $39\frac{3}{4} \times 29\frac{5}{8}$ (101 × 75). Gift of the Celeste and Armand Bartos Foundation

150 Richard Hamilton
(b. 1922), *Interior*, 1964.
Serigraph, $19\frac{5}{16} \times 25\frac{1}{8}$
($49 \times 63 \cdot 8$). Gift of Mrs.
Joseph M. Edinburg

prints during the 1960s, while often inspired by common objects such as money and cigar boxes, never released the viewer from his *148* subjective involvement, which was considered inessential in Pop art. Unlike the Pop artists who froze and made absolutely inert any vestige of lifelikeness in their subjects, Rivers tended to humanize the most inanimate object.

Jim Dine, twelve years younger than Rivers, was captivated by the manufactured object. He knew that objects had considerable power within themselves to control and change lives. In the 1950s Dine was one of the first creators of 'Happenings,' the form of participation theater in which visual elements and their manipulation took precedence over dialogue. In his *Car Crash* happening, rolls of bandages, headlights and other symbolic objects became the chorus to a tragedy in which the human participants assumed the roles of the destructive objects. In his print *Eleven Part Self Portrait (Red Pony)* (1965), executed *149* at Universal Limited Art Editions, a bathrobe becomes the personality of the artist, its various parts numbered to expand the object beyond its discrete form. Dine's penchant for watercolor and its seductive quality is apparent in the use of *tusche* in this lithograph. It is perhaps because Dine is also a poet that even the most banal objects (his subjects have included awls, false teeth, striped ties, hammers, and chisels) are imbued with a humanistic sympathy quite unlike the cool detachment of most Pop art.

175

The objectives of Pop art were most clearly set forth by the British artist, Richard Hamilton, both in his writings and in his paintings and prints. While the artistic situation in Great Britain was quite different from that in America, the awakening to mid-twentieth-century culture was nearly simultaneous in the two countries. Hamilton looked to the glossy pages of American movie and health-fad magazines, the sensuous hard-sell advertisements aimed at a newly affluent middle-class society, and the heavy-handed sexuality of all the popular media. In 1957 he put together a list of characteristics that underlie the philosophy of Pop art and that tended to be manifest in his own work as well as that of Lichtenstein and Warhol: 'Popular (designed for a mass audience), transient (short-term solution), expendable (easily forgotten), low cost, mass-produced, young (aimed at youth), witty, sexy, gimmicky, glamorous, big business.'[31] Hamilton's first print in this vein was a silkscreen that recapitulated the type of collage paintings that inaugurated the Pop movement in the late 1950s. This print, *Interior* (1964), combined clippings from maga-zines juxtaposed in a jagged, illogical manner which tended to elicit a

150

151 Friedrich Hundertwasser (Friedrich Stowasser) (b. 1928), *Goodbye to Africa*, 1967. Lithograph, $18\frac{1}{2} \times 24\frac{5}{8}$ (47 × 62·5). Purchase

152 Enrico Baj (b. 1924), *The Archduke Charles at the Battle of Aspern-Essling*, 1965. Etching, $11\frac{3}{4} \times 9\frac{5}{8}$ (29·8 × 24·4). Mrs. Alfred R. Stern Fund

satirical viewing of their now revealed 'hidden persuaders.' Hamilton was one of the first artists to be highly sensitive to photographic manipulation and used the commercially developed methods of photography, particularly personality-erasing fashion camera work, to create his own imagery. This was a direction he took in his silk-screen (or screen print, as the British prefer, having long substituted synthetic fabric for silk) of Frank Lloyd Wright's Guggenheim Museum (*The 'Solomon R. Guggenheim*, 1965). Hamilton took his view of the museum from a picture postcard sent to him by the British Pop movement's most amiable critic, Lawrence C. Alloway, then the museum's curator. The spiraling floors of the building and the poor color reproduction of the pale beige paint that covers the entire exterior inspired Hamilton. He saw the form as an architectural equivalent of a spirally stitched woman's brassiere, and interpreted the color as flesh-pink. It was only left to him to manipulate the postcard reproduction, touching it up as one might a fashion photograph to simplify the planes, curves, and shadows, and 'beefing-up' the color. The result is a composition as tightly constructed as any of Léger's,

153

giving an object that has its own well-known identity the sort of cosmetic treatment that has become part of our visual culture.

The inert and immutable construction of Pop-art compositions is most clearly viewed in the works of Roy Lichtenstein. This American artist, a year younger than Hamilton, had sought a means of creating the sort of incredible jigsaw-perfect composition that was the ideal of objective Abstractionists. His view of art was strictly formalist, without any commitment to comment upon the contemporary nature of things. It was accidental that he found his best 'unified pattern of seeing' [32] in the compositions of contemporary comic strips, even though this coincided so well with the subjects of Pop art. However, the comic-strip paintings and prints which characterize Lichtenstein's work of the early 1960s are selected frames from myriads of possibilities, which he has altered in color, relationship of masses, and so on. This burden of choice, whatever his aim, undeniably could not have been taken up without some attitude outside of traditional formalism. It is worth noting that Lichtenstein and Andy Warhol chose at the same time to take comic strips as their subject, and Warhol, being younger and less committed to the images he found in the comics, looked for different material after he discovered this conflict. The essential formal elements of the color comic strip that Lichtenstein took into his work consisted of solid black outlines surrounding areas of color, either totally flat and unvaried or made up of the ready-made dots (Ben Day dots) used to create lighter tones for the reproductive process utilized on newspaper or magazine comic-strip pages.

153 Richard Hamilton (b. 1922), *The Solomon R. Guggenheim*, 1965. Serigraph, 22 × 22 (55·8 × 55·8). Joseph G. Mayer Foundation Fund

154 Andy Warhol
(1930–1987), *Marilyn*
from *Ten Marilyns*. New
York, Castelli, 1967.
Serigraph, 36 × 36
(91·4 × 91·4). Gift of
David Whitney

Unmodulated black and primary colors were best achieved through the stencil process, and in making prints Lichtenstein used silkscreen to its best advantage. The sharp edges and persistent dots had a mechanical precision that would have been sacrificed in a less stable medium. A Lichtenstein silkscreen such as *Sweet Dreams, Baby!* (or *Pow!*), from *Eleven Pop Artists* (1965), viewed in terms of its composition rather than its subjective content, is successful because the medium clearly defines its highly organized structure. When the artist turned to lithography at Gemini's studio, his work consisted of creating stencils for the transfer of his images to the plates and stones, a process not far removed from silkscreen, which had previously been solely a tool of commercial lithography.

156

One cannot, however, write about the silkscreen as the dominant medium of Pop art without citing its major proponent, Andy Warhol. Warhol started his career as a commercial artist, creating advertisements for shoes in a highly personal and whimsical style. His decision to become a serious artist coincided with the new enthusiasm for American art among people in the women's fashion business. Attempt-

155 Jasper Johns (b. 1930), *Ale Cans*, 1964. Lithograph, $14\frac{1}{4} \times 11\frac{3}{16}$ (36·2 × 28·4). Gift of the Celeste and Armand Bartos Foundation

ing and discarding several themes and techniques, he turned to the silkscreen as the medium by which he was to create images both on canvas and on paper. He combined two methods: flat solid-colored shapes that utilized the basic stencil feature of silkscreen and extremely enlarged reproductions of photographs that were imposed on the screen photographically. Using the stencil style alone, Warhol produced his series of Campbell soup can paintings and prints and his Ajax boxes, reproducing everyday objects in a new form and scale, thereby making them at once visible and mysterious subjects.

In essence, Warhol was a portrait artist, all his work sharing the intense and ravishing spotlight of examination that fixed the exterior form into the shape of the personality within. His many
154 canvases and prints of Marilyn Monroe, the movie star whose life and suicide made her an epic figure of the 1960s, consisted of the same

156 Roy Lichtenstein (b. 1923), *Sweet Dreams, Baby!* (*Pow!*) from *Eleven Pop Artists*. New York, Original Editions, 1965. Serigraph, $35\frac{3}{4} \times 25\frac{9}{16}$ (90·8 × 65). Gift of Original Editions

photograph of her face, taken from a reproduction in which the dots of the process used create the blacks and grays. This photograph is enlarged to such an extent that one becomes aware that the areas of dots are nothing more than references to eyes, hair, and mouth. Added to this abstracted but recognizable photo- or real-portrait is a stencil portrait made up of flat shapes that seem to refer mainly to the false or superficial elements of the star's face: lipstick, eyeshadow, wig, and so forth. Warhol used the silkscreen as a mechanical and anonymous collaborator, allowing the medium to define his intent. Marshall McLuhan's interpretations of mid-twentieth-century culture in terms of the various forms or media of communication drew considerable attention during the 1960s. Warhol's work was probably the closest contemporary visual evocation of McLuhan's controversial declaration: 'The medium is the message.'

An integral part of Pop art was the proliferation of its images. Not only did the inspiration for their subjects come from the mass-oriented commercial media, but the Pop artists emulated the blanketing effect successfully used by advertisers to sell their products. Uniqueness, that aspect of art so deeply ingrained in its appreciation in modern times, was a suspect quality discarded by some of the Pop artists. Andy Warhol consistently reprinted his images so that, for example, there were over three thousand canvases and portfolios of prints of his *Flowers*. But the Pop image that held the record for dissemination – to the extent that it became as well known throughout the U.S.A. as some major commercial products – was Robert Indiana's *157* *LOVE*. First painted on canvas in 1965, the four letters of the word 'LOVE' were arranged in a square and brightly colored. Indiana's vision of the American dream was found in the signs advertising its components, such as 'EAT' on a roadside restaurant. This area of inspiration was not his alone, since most of the Pop artists in the early 1960s had isolated one word ('ART' was the most popular) in paintings or constructions, drawing to it the silent veneration expected of the serious art appreciator. *LOVE* became the image for the 'hippie' generation, who, in a period when discussion centred on the premise 'God is dead,' needed a universal spiritual sign. While the idea of love was expanding and being redefined, the symbol Indiana devised along the lines of a business logotype became a limited edition print (several times in various colors), was pirated for commercial production as posters, was made into a chromed metal multiple, was en-

157 Robert Indiana (b. 1928), *German Love* from *Graphik USA*, 1968. Serigraph, $22\frac{1}{8} \times 22\frac{1}{16}$ (56·5 × 56·2). John B. Turner Fund

larged into a mammoth steel sculpture, and, finally, was engraved and issued as an official United States postage stamp in 1973, well after the love generation had grown up.

James Rosenquist was formerly a billboard sign painter, who found in the residue of overlapping commercial advertisements a combination of ready-made or found-object imagery and contemporary subject-matter. In his earliest lithographs made at Universal's workshop, he experimented with non-fine-art means to achieve his disjointed and distorted compositions, using spraygun and patterned wallpaint rollers. He later went on to create ambitious multipanel reinterpretations of his large environmental paintings, such as *Horse Blinders* (1973) and *F-111* (1974). These giant compositions skillfully combine silkscreen and lithography for broad and vibrant-colored effects. Characteristically, Rosenquist presents a segment of a pictorial representation of an object in magnified form. *Forehead I* (1968) 158 incorporates the oversized billboard forms to achieve a somewhat disoriented and shattering effect. Rosenquist's work recapitulates the basic derivative nature of Pop art using disparate subject-matter from the purely commercial arena. His pictorial usage also depends

183

upon a hitherto unexpected but constantly visible source – the collage of billboard signs.

In Great Britain, there were several artists who followed a similar path. Foremost among them were the sculptor Eduardo Paolozzi and an American painter living abroad, R. B. Kitaj. Both chose to compose their silkscreens in a serial manner, creating compositions that were mélanges of incongruous forms and objects. Paolozzi had spent the late 1940s studying Jean Dubuffet's collection of primitive art. He also felt the influence of the Surrealists, and some of his work evokes memories of Max Ernst's collages for *Une Semaine de Bonté* (1934). Paolozzi's sculpture of the late 1950s consisted of figures constructed of metal cast from industrial forms. The figures had a robot-like appearance, and most of the human forms in his prints share this mechanistic tendency; if not, they draw upon the stylized figures of medical books. In his first major suite of prints, *As Is When* (1965), based on the life and philosophy of Ludwig Wittgenstein, Paolozzi provides most of the pictorial material from which he was to compose his prints during the following decade. Not only are there machines and dehumanized human objects, but a large amount of geometric form is included to assert a species of structure upon the disparate objects. However, the structure in *Wittgenstein in New York* (*As Is When*, 1965) is no more informative of the way the composition

159

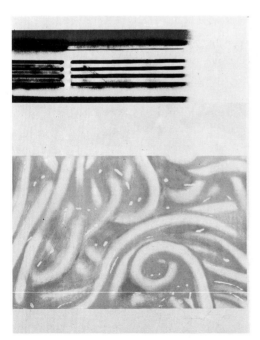

158 (*left*) Jim Rosenquist (b. 1933), *Forehead I*, 1968. Lithograph, $28\frac{7}{16} \times 24\frac{9}{16}$ ($72\cdot2 \times 62\cdot3$). John B. Turner Fund

159 (*right*) Eduardo Paolozzi (b. 1924), *Wittgenstein in New York* from *As is When*. London, Editions Alecto, 1965. Serigraph, $30 \times 21\frac{1}{8}$ ($76 \times 53\cdot6$). The Joseph G. Mayer Foundation Fund

160 (*far right*) R. B. Kitaj (b. 1932), *World Ruin Through Black Magic*, 1963. Serigraph, $49\frac{3}{8} \times 34\frac{5}{8}$ ($125\cdot4 \times 89$). John B. Turner Fund

should be interpreted than if it did not exist. In fact it adds a de-defining element, much as Rauschenberg's obliterating brush strokes did. The insistent color patterns in Paolozzi's work also refer to sources in scientific illustration, so that the viewer once again is presented with 'artified' visual information recovered and turned into art itself.

Kitaj, who also utilizes a geometric structure to codify his selection of forms, has a far more literary point of departure. The insertion of quotations and names encourages the viewer to work out a theme that encompasses all the variety of disconnected visual material offered. In the large, complex, collage-generated screen print *World Ruin* 160 *Through Black Magic* (1963), it is nearly impossible to ignore the inference of the title as it applies to the pictorial elements of the composition. The application of a restrictive structure to the collage format was a sign that some manner of serial viewing was demanded, and Kitaj went further into the serialization of his objects by creating a portfolio, *In Our Time* (1969), of fifty screen prints of book covers. While the screen-print process transformed the photoimages of the book covers, the selective process (the books were from Kitaj's library) was extended by placing the magnified image of each book without any compositional additions on a large sheet of white paper. These fifty prints provide a cumulative experience activated by the viewer's recollection.

Neither Kitaj nor Paolozzi could have produced their elaborate

early silkscreens without the expertise of Christopher Prater. In 1963 the Institute of Contemporary Arts in London commissioned Richard Hamilton, David Hockney, Paolozzi, Bridget Riley, and other British artists to create screen prints at Prater's Kelpra Studio. Before the I.C.A. project Prater had been a commercial printer with only one assistant and had rarely worked with artists. After the project Kelpra became the hub of British printmaking activity, as Hamilton, Paolozzi, and Kitaj posed problems, particularly in the use of photo-mechanical techniques, that Prater imaginatively solved. The silkscreen seemed to dominate printmaking during the 1960s in Great Britain.

England provided a fertile situation for Pop artists like Allen Jones, whose interest in the commercially contrived and artificial manipulation of the female form to accentuate its sex-signaling factors coincided with a series of scandals involving prostitutes and members of the British government. One of the subjects that Jones used extensively in his prints was the exaggerated stiletto-heeled shoe that characterized sexy lingerie advertisements and the dragon-ladies of the comic books. The manner in which humans allowed themselves to become deformed by commercial stratagem was only one of many subjects for the Pop artist who was recording elements of an environment that no longer consisted only of trees, boulevards, and boating parties.

The changes in the daily habits of society were part of the Pop artists' documentation, so while David Hockney has much in common with the post-World War II figurative artists, he brings to his

161 Allen Jones (b. 1937), *Green Yellow*, 1966. Lithograph, 30 × 22¼ (76·2 × 56·5). Gift of Kleiner, Bell and Co.

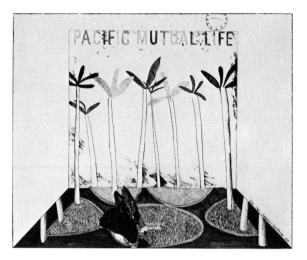

162 David Hockney (b. 1937), *Pacific Mutual Life Building with Palm Trees*, 1964. Lithograph, 20$\frac{3}{16}$ × 25 (51·3 × 63·5). Gift of Kleiner, Bell and Co.

paintings and prints the detachment of the census taker. His human beings rest in their compositions with the same immutability as objects in a still life. Hockney's etchings, in particular, are composed of dry lines, somewhat tentative and chaste, depicting a static and dispassionate scene. Often a member of the so-called 'jet set,' Hockney found many of his best images in southern California, which had become another center for Pop-oriented art. The Hollywood life-   *162* style of flashy cars, endless throughways, roadside restaurants, sun 'worship,' and frenetic product consumption, as well as the influential movie industry fostered a particularly trenchant form of Pop art through the overwhelming presence of trite imagery. Because of the presence of several print workshops, nearly all the California Pop artists made prints. Some who produced interesting printed images were Mel Ramos, Ed Ruscha, and Wayne Thiebaud.

A large group of educated young urbanites who earned excellent wages well before they began to raise families provided the audience for Pop art and an increasingly active market for Pop prints. Most of the artists were asked to produce prints by the many publishers who sought to take advantage of their popularity, but not all the artists showed a deep interest in or commitment to the print media. Peter Blake, Alan D'Arcangelo, Claes Oldenburg, Peter Phillips, and Tom Wesselmann are only a few American and British Pop artists who made significant prints (mainly silkscreen and improved offset processes) during the print boom of the 1960s.

It was inevitable that some part of the Pop artists' attitude toward

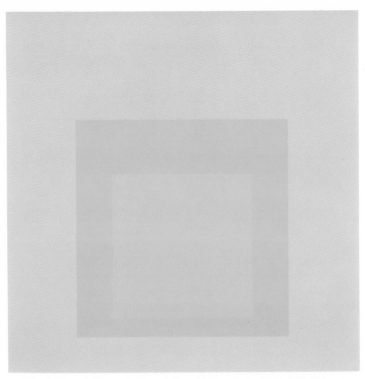

163 Josef Albers (1888–1976), plate V from *Homage to the Square: Midnight and Noon*, 1964. Lithograph, $15\frac{3}{4} \times 15\frac{7}{8}$ (40 × 40·3). Gift of Kleiner, Bell and Co.

the object would also be shared by artists in other countries where there was an invasion of American commercialism. While the Pop strain was weak in Continental Europe, similar beginnings were made using found objects, from old-fashioned and nostalgic ephemera to contemporary trash. In France the main adherents of New Realism, Yves Klein, Jean Tinguely, and Arman, were not at all involved in the print media in the early 1960s. Well after Klein's death in 1962, Arman, Tinguely and his wife Niki de Saint-Phalle, and a young Bulgarian member, Christo, were eventually persuaded to create prints. Arman's encased accumulations of similar or identical objects have a formal emphasis far more attached to classic European compositional tradition than to the neo-Dadaist attitude of the American Pop artist. Tinguely's prints celebrated his self-destructing machines by recording his diabolical plans in the various media. Saint-Phalle's *Nanas* ('broads'), superficially derived from folk-art motifs

188

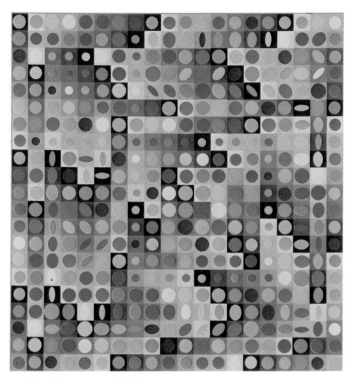

164 (*above*) Victor Vasarely (b. 1908),
plate 2 from *Planetary Folklore*.
Cologne, Galerie Der Spiegel, 1964.
Serigraph, $25\frac{9}{16} \times 24\frac{7}{16}$ (65×62).
Larry Aldrich Fund

165 Richard Anuszkiewicz (b. 1930),
plate 3 from *The Inward Eye* by William
Blake. Baltimore, Aquarius Press, 1970.
Serigraph, $25\frac{3}{4} \times 19\frac{7}{8}$ ($65 \cdot 4 \times 50 \cdot 5$).
Purchase

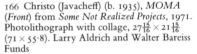

166 Christo (Javacheff) (b. 1935), *MOMA (Front)* from *Some Not Realized Projects*, 1971. Photolithograph with collage, $27\frac{15}{16} \times 21\frac{15}{16}$ (71×55.8). Larry Aldrich and Walter Bareiss Funds

166

(as preserved in carnival sculpture), are among the first manifestations in art of the rising female consciousness and the movement for women's liberation. Christo's wrapped objects, landscapes, and buildings are quite the opposite of what even the assemblagists attempted. While the latter made the psychologically invisible common objects in their environment once again visible by putting them in a new context, Christo, in both three-dimensional and printed works, wrapped and made familiar things obscure, so that it was necessary to activate memories of the concealed objects.

Arman, Tinguely, and Saint-Phalle were among the artists who contributed works to the first 'multiple' art project, MAT (Multiplication of Transformable Art). Organized by the Swiss artists Karl Gerstner and Daniel Spoerri, the group of three-dimensional objects in editions appeared in 1959. Included was a book of geometrically cut sheets, which could be rearranged to form several compositions, made by their compatriot Dietrich Roth (then using the pseudonym Diter Rot). Like Spoerri, Roth was interested in a form of assemblage focused on remains rather than on selections. Roth's random accretions of compositional ideas have produced a large body of graphic and multiple work, often in unorthodox media and in collaboration with other artists.

190

11 Op, kinetic, Concrete, and the Conceptual arts

ALL THROUGH THE HEYDAY of Abstract Expressionism and then of Pop art the geometric abstract tradition of Constructivism and De Stijl had continued to exist. Never entirely an underground situation, this area of abstract art survived in the practice of design and the study of composition and color theory when it lacked a congenial audience. In the U.S.A. Josef Albers continued to teach, occasionally making prints recapitulating in embossed and uninked line his con- stellations of illusion-provoking geometric constructions. These prints of the 1950s, entitled *Intaglio Duo A, B, C*, and so on, preceded 169 the work of several artists who made inkless embossed prints in both geometric form (the Canadian Yves Gaucher) and Pop (the Colom- bian Omar Rayo).

While Albers's constellations can be traced back to the artist's work at the Bauhaus, his most important explorations in post-World War II years were in the field of color. Working on paintings serially titled *Homage to the Square*, Albers codified his theory of color (*Interaction of Color*, Yale, 1963) a year after he created his first litho- graphs in the form given to his paintings. The second set of litho- graphs Albers made at Tamarind Workshop, *Homage to the Square:* 163 *Midnight and Noon* (1964), were among the earliest works to demon- strate that the close relationships of color needed to produce the illusions of aura and change of dimension could be successfully ob- tained in print media. Until this point Matisse's *pochoirs* for *Jazz* were the sole examples of compositions whose spatial contrasts were produced largely through the contiguity of areas of highly saturated flat color. The print media, particularly lithography and silkscreen, lent themselves well to artists who, like Albers, sought to compose their paintings from unmodulated color. In the case of many artists of the 1950s and 1960s, this meant obtaining optical effects through

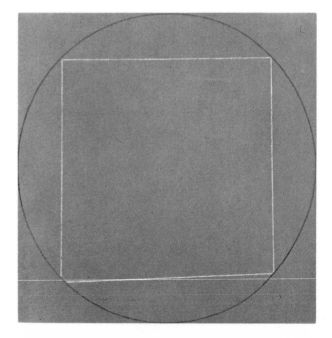

167 (*above*) Ellsworth Kelly (b.
1923), *Blue/Green*, 1970.
Lithograph, $25\frac{13}{16} \times 27\frac{3}{4}$
($65 \cdot 5 \times 70 \cdot 5$). Gift of Connie and
Jack Glenn, Pinky and Arthur
Kase

168 Robert Mangold (b. 1937),
plate 1 from *7 Aquatints*. New
York, Parasol Press, 1973.
Aquatint, $15\frac{5}{8} \times 15\frac{11}{16}$ ($39 \cdot 6 \times 39 \cdot 8$).
John B. Turner Fund

169 Josef Albers (1888–1976), *Intaglio Duo B*, 1958. Inkless intaglio, $5\frac{1}{16} \times 13\frac{11}{16}$ (12·8 × 34·7). Gift of Mr. and Mrs. Armand P. Bartos

the interaction of hues placed in serial arrangements that would enhance the illusions sought. Others dealt with expansive planes of color, creating tension and the appearance of spatial contrast through the confrontation of their sharp edges. The optical group found its roots in Constructivism and the design formulae of the Bauhaus, while the aspirations of the second group tended to branch out from the paths of Synthetic Cubism and the less rigidly systematic among the Abstraction-Creation artists of the 1930s.

The most prominent of the design-based optical artists to create a large corpus of prints has been Victor Vasarely, who had studied in his native Hungary with a former Bauhaus student. He has theorized that the integration and inseparability of form and color, which he calls 'plastic unity,' provides the basis for the construction of infinite numbers of compositions. In most of his works the grouping of units creates contrasts of form and color that stimulate a visual sense of spatial movement. A typical example of his work of the 1960s is his album entitled *Planetary Folklore* (1964), in which large squares *164* made up of hundreds of binary units (each consisting of a geometric form within a square) in contrasting colors present quite complex illusory effects. Vasarely has had a social message in mind as he developed his compositional ideas: If the content of art consisted purely of color and simple geometric forms, the viewer would not have to bring to its appreciation a personal life-experience. Thus, it has been Vasarely's intention to expand his compositions into architectural components and insure wider distribution of them not only as silkscreen prints but also by manufacturing multiple units with which the possessor could create his own compositions.

Among the many artists whose prints have kinetic possibilities in their disposition of color are several who followed the lead of another Bauhaus-trained artist, the Swiss architect, designer, painter, and sculptor Max Bill. In 1936 Bill had formulated a definition in which works of Concrete art originated 'on the basis of means and laws of their own, without external reliance on natural phenomena or any transformation of them.'[33] In addition, Vasarely and other members of the Denise René Gallery in Paris, who were devoted to pure abstraction or Concrete art, drew many young Latin Americans to their theories. The Argentine Julio LeParc, the Brazilian Almire Mavignier, and the Venezuelans Jesus Rafael Soto and Carlos Cruz-Diez, have all made prints that rely on geometric form and color to produce sensations of movement. The New Tendency exhibitions in Zagreb, devoted to this artistic concern, also showed the prints of the Italians Getulio Alviani and Alberto Biasi, the Frenchman François Morellet, and the Yugoslav Ivan Picelj. Several of these artists added a third dimension to their two-dimensional compositions by printing them on sheets of plexiglass and combining two or more sheets, so that the spectator's own movement in relation to the work sets up its kinetic effect. This was one of the many ways these and other artists concerned with light and movement extended the print into three-dimensionality.

Few artists from the U.S.A. were exclusively concerned with optical sensation. Richard Anuszkiewicz, a student of Albers, has been the one most faithful to this form of art and has created many silk-screens which rely on extremely bright colors in paneled compositions, each panel filled with thin lines of contrasting color, activating the spectator's photokinetic response. In his illustrations to William Blake's *The Inward Eye* (Baltimore, Aquarius Press, 1970) Anuszkiewicz has used an art of no external references to extend the literary references. The work of Ad Reinhardt is more difficult to classsify, since his use of slightly varied tones of black produced an almost invisible geometric pattern, thus making his art perhaps more minimal than kinetic. Before his death in 1967 he created one series of silkscreens, which failed, technically, to reproduce the subtle transitions of his paintings.

Other retinal artists using color have dealt with the halo effect (Wojciech Fangor) and have attempted to convey the physical sensation of afterimage (Otto Piene). Contrast, perhaps the most

165

170 Pol Bury (b. 1922), plate X from *X Cinetizations*. New York, Lefebre, 1966. Serigraph, $19\frac{9}{16} \times 14\frac{11}{16}$ ($51 \cdot 5 \times 37$). Gift of Mr. and Mrs. John Lefebre

171 Fritz Glarner (1899–1972), *Drawing for Tondo*, 1959. Lithograph, $14\frac{5}{16} \times 13\frac{13}{16}$ ($36 \cdot 3 \times 35$). Gift of the Celeste and Armand Bartos Foundation

vivifying element in this form of art, does not require color to set up its effects. The black and white screen prints of the British painter Bridget Riley generated vertigo and other strong physiological reactions to their moiré and other disorienting patterns. Pol Bury, the Belgian whose sculptures move in slow and unexpected sequences, *170* cut photographs into concentric circles, and moved each circular band slightly so that the finished, printed composition showed the subject askew in a completely bewildering manner. The production of such optical tricks, particularly in silkscreen, has been widespread, and the kinetic print, more than any other style except pure geometrical abstraction, proliferated in the 1960s.

The rage for nonobjective prints (they were the ideal substitute for reproductions, historical prints, and other decorations in glass-walled office buildings during this period) even revived interest in the compositions of older artists whose styles had elicited the newer forms. Sonia Delaunay, for example, created several lithographs and aquatints during the 1960s which recapitulate Orphist imagery of fifty years earlier. Mondrian, who was never to make a print in his abstract style, nevertheless exerted an influence on abstract printmaking after

195

172 Alexander Calder
(1898–1976), *Red Sun*,
1965. Lithograph,
$20\frac{7}{16} \times 27\frac{1}{2}$ (52 × 69·8). John
B. Turner Fund

World War II. His association with the Abstraction-Creation group in
Paris in 1931 and his exile in the U.S.A. during the war made his role
pivotal for two American artists: the sculptor Alexander Calder and
the Swiss-born painter Fritz Glarner. Calder had been a member of the
Abstraction-Creation group and had created his first mobiles the
year it was formed. His combination of movement and bright color
did not become the subject of his prints until the late 1940s. In his
172 prints of the 1960s few totally abstract compositions occur, but the
flat, brilliant red and black that dominate Calder's lithographs are
their structure as well. Mondrian's limited palette and right-angled
forms were the basis of the work of his most direct disciple, Glarner.
Glarner, also a member of the Abstraction-Creation group, translated
171 Mondrian's primary colors and grays into circular compositions in
which the strict verticals and horizontals were wedged apart by
diagonal panels. It is to Glarner's lithographs that one must look for
the type of print Mondrian undoubtedly would have created, for
they are sensitive, searching crayon lithographs in which Glarner
has chronicled, line by line, the formation of his compositions.
With his friend Max Bill, Glarner was utterly devoted to the construction of harmonious structures of geometric forms.

In Europe, as has been seen, two generations carried geometric
abstraction into prints: Max Bill, Richard P. Lohse, and Auguste
Herbin were the older masters of the genre; Jean Dewasne and
Richard Mortensen were representative of the postwar group who

196

participated in the Salon des Réalités Nouvelles, increasingly making of it a forum for the Concretist artists. This 'cool' art form with its unmuddied colors strongly contrasted with the concurrent Expressionist abstraction. Its content appealed to those wary of the motivations and meanings behind the emotional surges of line and color in 'l'art autre' as Michel Tapié called it. Eventually art students exposed to both factions made choices. One of the more interesting results of the influence of Geometric Abstraction is found in the work of the American Ellsworth Kelly. He worked in Paris longer than most Americans (1948–54), and he returned to a New York ringing with action painting. He developed a style in which color and form, with antecedents in the works of Matisse and Arp, became shaped into geometricized compositions. This has meant unusual-shaped or compartmentalized canvases in his paintings, and parallelograms, *167* ellipses and other geometrical forms in brilliant color or black floating on large, unmodulated areas of white in his prints. Kelly's lithographs, made in both Paris and Los Angeles, are excellent examples of the direction abstract art took in the 1960s. They are outstanding because of his sense of perfection, which, like Albers's, is intuitive in regard to color balance. The so-called 'hard edges' of the color forms as they meet each other are not barriers but rather interacting planes that inaugurate rhythms and tensions.

Only a few of the American painters of the later 1960s concerned with regulated structure and color have made successful prints. One, Frank Stella, worked in both lithography and silkscreen when he *173* produced series of prints, in small format, which essentially

173 Frank Stella (b. 1936), *Quathlamba I* from *V Series*, 1968. Lithograph, 11 1/16 × 25 7/8 (28 × 65·7). John B. Turner Fund

documented his earlier paintings; in some cases they have the wall-carrying properties of the paintings, even at one-eighth the size of those canvases. The shaped canvases of Stella's paintings found their contours from an interior structure of parallel bands in geometric patterns. In print, Stella related the white paper to a wall upon which his composition rested as well as to a negative space. This attempt to convey in print form the same relationship that exists between a painting and its environment, or between a mural and its host wall, has entailed certain changes in esthetic sensitivity. A German artist, Palermo, created interior environments within galleries by painting each wall. One room might have a band of color running its length, another would have the structure of each wall altered by the geometric form painted upon it. His prints, in turn, documented the forms painted on the wall without reference to scale or surroundings.

A grid of intersecting lines became, in the 1960s, the ultimate geometric composition. The paintings done between 1960 and 1967 by the Canadian-born Agnes Martin had no printed equivalents until the 1970s, when she created a series of silkscreen prints, *On a* 174 *Clear Day* (New York, Parasol Press, 1973), which were manufactured by Luitpold Domberger in Stuttgart after her mathematically annotated sketches. Having removed herself from the craft area of creation, Martin was able to insure the precision that was basic to the evocation of a mathematical/meditational response. The gray grids of thirty different interior proportions, for all their apparent exactitude, are none the less intuitively conceived. Other artists who express themselves through the exact terms of geometric forms have, like the Cubists of many decades before, found etching to be the ideal medium. The clearest examples in the print media of the Ameri- 176 can Conceptual artist Sol LeWitt's serial statements appear in the line etchings he has done at Crown Point Press in California. He has taken his linear projections which, in their most monumental form, are drawn directly onto walls, and etched them onto plates of traditional scale and proportion. The relatively simple systems, generally developed from straight lines in black or in primary colors, have served as the basis for a great number of prints that incorporate minimal, consistently pure geometric statements. The British artist 175 Richard Smith and the American painter Robert Mangold both created etchings in which geometrical distortion is a distinguishing factor. Smith, who most often created layered prints with bent and cut

198

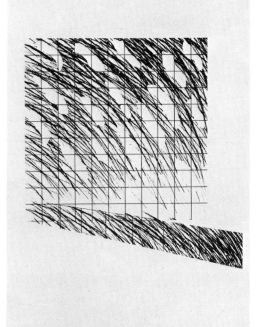

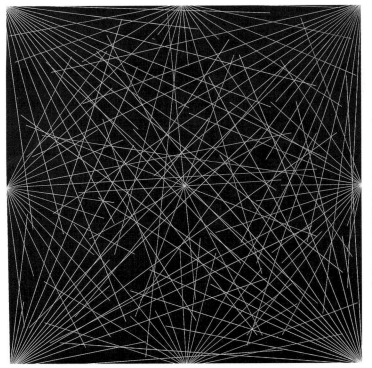

174 Agnes Martin (b. 1912), plate 18 from
On a Clear Day. New York, Parasol Press,
1973. Serigraph, $7\frac{1}{2} \times 6\frac{3}{4}$ (19 × 17). Gift of
the artist and Parasol Press, Ltd.

175 Richard Smith (b. 1931), *Proscenium I*,
1971. Etching, $20\frac{3}{8} \times 19\frac{1}{2}$ (51·7 × 49·5).
Reiss-Cohen Fund

176 Sol LeWitt
(b. 1928), *Lines from
Sides, Corners and
Center*, 1977. Etching
and aquatint, printed
in color, $34\frac{5}{8} \times 34\frac{7}{8}$
(87.9 × 88.5). Gift of
Barbara Pine
(through the
Associates of the
Department of Prints
and Illustrated Books)

177 Gerhard Richter
(b. 1932), plate 4 from
Canary Landscapes, 1971.
Photoengraving and
aquatint, $11\frac{11}{16} \times 15\frac{3}{4}$
(29·6 × 40). Gift of Mrs.
Carol O. Selle

175   portions emulating his shaped canvases, offers the geometric foundation for such contorted structures in his gritty etchings. Mangold
combines in his prints confusing irregular arrangements of squares and
168   circles. His colors in the 1970s were extremely muted, but their
tendency to dullness is obviated by the granular surface of aquatint,
which reflects rather than absorbs light.

The use of the intaglio techniques, particularly aquatint, increased
in the 1970s. In the late 1960s Jasper Johns made a portfolio at
Universal Limited Art Editions in which his own etched plates were
printed on the same sheet as photoengravings of his sculpture. In a
second state he added aquatint to the etchings and etched lines to the
photoengravings. In 1972 the American painter of totally white
canvases, Robert Ryman, made ivory-white aquatints in which the
density of the ink and its contoured edges as it approaches the edge of
the plate are the only sensible variables. Ryman's prints provoke the
viewer to sense infinitesimal variations, thus shifting awareness from
abstract imagery to physical reality.

Almost all of the forms taken by art that derive from the
impositions of systems of organization, from Albers through LeWitt,
obtain their impetus from a heightened awareness of process. Albers,
who consciously preferred mechanical instruments and standard paint
colors, passed on his Bauhaus philosophy to artists who also wished to
remove the personal and unpredictable from their works. By the late

200

1960s, however, there was also a feeling that all the possible forms of Western art had been explored. What was left except to examine the processes by which it was made? LeWitt incorporated instructions into his works, often executed by others; another American artist, Jennifer Bartlett, created forms from the sizes of dots and other simple marks filled into the squares of her grids.

In print there were many techniques through which artists could exploit this subject: the gradual deterioration of a copper plate exposed to acid was the basis of one work by the English artist Tom Phillips; the surface of paper and its retention of a process that affected both recto and verso, such as embossing, became the subject of many years' work by the Japanese artist, Shoichi Ida.

While emphasizing such procedures in printmaking, it was inevitable that the crafts allied to it would be exploited as well. Considerable attention was given to paper, and with the growing population of young people who wanted independence and sought it in artistic pursuits, this was a fresh medium, without too many constricting precedents. Workshops for papermaking were set up, both to produce uniform runs of specially colored and textured sheets for prints as well as to allow artists to create in the medium of paper. Mention is made of this efflorescence of what is essentially a craft because several prominent artists made editions of paper works in association with the workshops of printers. Ken Tyler's work, beginning in 1974 with Robert Rauschenberg, and continuing later with Frank Stella, David Hockney and Richard Smith, developing molds and stencils that organized colored paper pulp into compositions, came out of his experiments in the printshop.

The same period experienced a shift in the opposite direction: the viewer was offered works exhibiting what seemed to be entirely realistic physicality and then asked to sense it abstractly. The New Realists (Hyperrealists or Photorealists) of the 1970s brought to their work in sculpture and painting the most acute sense of visuality. Pop art's transformation of photographic representation into paintings and prints was basically formalist. It found fundamental eccentricities in photoreproduction that determined the impression of realism that the public eye accepted. The younger and undeniably more technically sophisticated artist understands what the camera is incapable of capturing or eliminating. Examples of this form of realism may be found in the prints of the German Gerhard Richter and the American

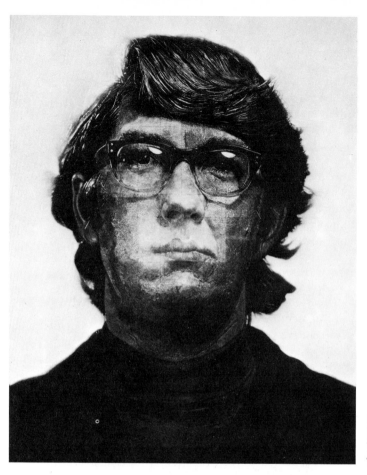

178 Chuck Close
(b. 1940), *Keith*, 1972.
Mezzotint, $45\frac{5}{8} \times 35\frac{1}{2}$
(116×90). John B.
Turner Fund

177 Chuck Close. Richter begins with photographic reality and blurs it, almost in the manner of those photographers who, in the nineteenth century, sought to attain in their new medium the effects Whistler created in his lithotints and etchings. Adding aquatint to photoengraved plates, Richter effectively extends a tourist-enticing landscape into a more sensuous realm of visual experience. By manipulating the various fields of focus and eliminating some elements that the camera, with its lack of detailed selectivity, could not remove, Richter offers a more 'real' view which remains, nevertheless, comfortably familiar and photographic. The mammoth portraits that Chuck Close has painted are created by a meticulously detailed brush technique after

photographs he has taken of his subject. For his first print, *Keith*, Close *178*
executed a grandiose mezzotint which, for one form of Photorealism,
should stand as the ultimate example. Unable to pit the entire 45 × 36
inch plate with the normal mezzotint tool with sufficient uniformity,
Close had the plate photographically etched to obtain the same
surface. Dividing the plate into one-inch-square areas, the artist
smoothed down the pits of each area manually, taking proofs at each
stage, so that by the time the edition was printed the earliest work had
begun to wear. In Close's mezzotint one can see the exact area of sharp
focus by its more visible contrast with blurred areas. Were it not for
the faint traces of the original one-inch grid, the photomechanical
reproduction here (small in scale and textured by the dots of the
reproduction process) could be confused with the photograph Close
used as his model.

The audience for this renaissance of realism was not one that found
comfort in all phases of the new art, although the possibility of actual
recognition drew to this art those who had no pleasure from abstract
forms. Besides Close, other Americans such as Richard Estes and *179*
Philip Pearlstein exploited the idea of intensely focussed realism. In his

179 Richard Estes (b. 1936),
Plate V from the portfolio
Urban Landscapes No. 2, 1979.
Silkscreen, printed in color,
$19\frac{7}{8} \times 13\frac{5}{16}$ (50.6 × 33.8). Gift
of a friend in memory of
Beth Lisa Feldman and
Wallace Reiss

very complicated silkscreens made with Domberger in Stuttgart, Estes accentuated the highly reflective surfaces of urban buildings. By including the kind of minutiae that the eye automatically disregards but the camera does not, he sets up a nearly abstract composition which must be analyzed in the same manner as a real, but visually confusing, situation. The preponderance of large canvases and Mme. Tussaud-style sculpture gave Hyperrealism an aura of the overpowering art, decoration, and relics of the Baroque church. The prints, for the most part, were mementos of paintings, executed almost exclusively with photographic techniques and thus paradoxically regenerating the photo-generated imagery of the unique works.

Apart from Photorealism, the photographic image has been a dominant part of certain forms of Conceptual art. This area has been almost exclusively documentary, so that series of photographs printed in offset or silkscreen become visual records of an artist's action or process. The techniques which make these informational pieces transferable to the print media inevitably eliminate a significant part of the photographic verisimilitude. Among the many artists who have issued prints in this form are the Canadians Iain Baxter and Les Levine, the Germans Wolf Vostell and Joseph Beuys and the British Keith Milow.

Basic to Conceptual art, of course, is the use of language. Some of the visual structures and techniques in printmaking used by artists who have subscribed to the limited ethos 'art is art' have been described. However, the most succinct definition of Conceptual art, 'inquiry into the foundations of the concept "art," as it has come to mean,'[34] given by Joseph Kosuth, requires a linguistic rather than plastic context. In describing some of the many stylistic tendencies in printmaking after World War II, only a few references have been made to the incidence of word imagery, graphism, or calligraphy. The use of or allusion to words in art is not a twentieth-century phenomenon. The development of letter forms as compositional elements without message-carrying properties, however, was part of the movement toward abstraction, but the beauty of a single letter of an alphabet was long ago recognized by the Oriental artist as well as the medieval illuminator. In the 1950s many artists chose to suggest writings of various forms in their paintings by transforming the design elements of letters. After the war a group in Paris dedicated to working in this manner called themselves 'Lettristes.' As artists found

180 Les Levine (b. 1935), *S29* from
Les Levine LXVI, 1966. Photo-offset,
12¾ × 9⁷⁄₁₆ (32·3 × 24). Gift of Fischbach
Gallery

more ideas in their commercialized environment, much of the
Lettrist painting became more literate, more informational, and more
readable. Throughout these postwar years, however, the primary
thrust of the imagery of letters and words was abstract. Even the Pop
words 'EAT' and 'LOVE' and the occasional message of protest were
artified by the addition of balancing compositional devices.

Divesting words of their intrinsic formal interest and returning
them, still within the context of visual art, to their principal role of
message bearing was the focus of many artists. The transitional artist
among those who recognized in language a plausible subject upon
which to build his paintings and prints was the Japanese Arakawa.
Utilizing stencil letters, as did Jasper Johns in his influential use of   *181*
words indicating placement, color, and title in his canvases and prints,
Arakawa poses philosophical problems in conjunction with pictorial
material. While some visual enjoyment is obtained from study of the
formal compositional elements, the words convey the substance of the
subject of the work. Unlike Johns, whose words are integral formal
elements that enhance or question their context, Arakawa inserts
nonverbal images as illustrations or indicators for the problems posed
in the lines of writing. Rather than allow the viewer to assume what

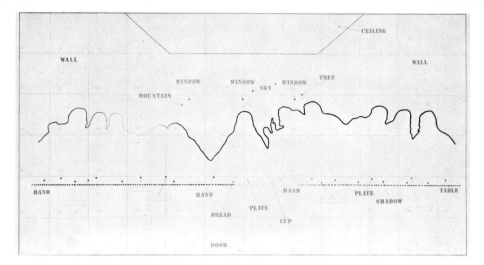

181 Arakawa (b. 1936), *Next to the Last*, 1971. Serigraph, $21\frac{1}{2} \times 41\frac{3}{4}$ (54·6 × 106). Reiss-Cohen Fund

the artist wishes to be experienced, the words are directives that may cast doubt upon what the images appear to convey.

The questioning of visual clues to reality is, of course, the oldest branch of philosophy. Abstract art tended to make the viewer more acutely sensitive to visual information. It is, therefore, logical that subsequent developments should return to questionable status that which our eyes have accepted as truth. Conceptual art, in its language form, dwells on meaning and, unlike Concrete poetry, with which it is often confused, is concerned more with the transformation of experience patterns than with interior linguistic manipulation. Thus, the purest examples of Conceptual art would be considered the work of Art & Language (the collaborative venture of several British artists, led by Terry Atkinson and Michael Baldwin, and later joined by the American Joseph Kosuth). Their project, begun in 1969, was confined to proposing visual problems through language alone. Besides magazines and exhibitions, they produced a series of prints, each expounding one area of a selected problem. Given the concentrated attention of art viewing, these prints, which resemble enlarged pages from any learned journal, alter expectations of immediate satisfaction, because they require a commitment of time related to reading rather than seeing.

It is impossible to complete the discussion of Conceptual Art without referring to one of its major by-products, the artist's book.

Earlier references have been made to the many deluxe editions illustrated or embellished by some of the foremost artists of this century with prints in the traditional media. The more casual booklets of the Russian Futurists included prints done in less elaborate ways which, none the less, are of major importance in the history of printmaking. The artist's book which flourished as an art form in the 1970s was a total art work, filled with words, photographs, drawings and collages. Its origins probably stem most directly from the various ephemeral publications of Fluxus, an international group of artists formed in the early 1960s.

These printed books were for many artists their only tangible expressions. Among the many creators of artist's books were Ed Ruscha, who pioneered the form in America in the 1960s with his photographic compendiums of parking lots and other Southern California sites, the Swiss artist Dietrich Roth, who produced a series of bound assemblages of found materials in addition to his geometric cut-out books, the Belgian Marcel Broodthaers, whose books borrowed the composition of French poetry publications and exhibition catalogues, the British performance artists Gilbert and George, who issued announcements and manifestos as well as books, such as one titled *Dark Shadows*, published in 1976, that gently reflected the mores of the local middle class, and Hamish Fulton, a Scotsman whose books have recorded his hikes across terrains all over the world. However, the most characteristic printing of the Conceptualist was in the form of text, reducing visual art to unembellished ideas.

In 1975 the Art and Language branch in New York founded a magazine, *The Fox*, in which the article, 'A Declaration of Independence' announced, 'At this point attempts to question or transform the nature of art beyond formalistic considerations must inevitably begin to involve a consideration not only of the presuppositions inherent in the internal structure of art models, but also a critical awareness of the social system which preconditions and drastically confines the possibility of transformation.'[35] This new Marxist interpretation of the role of art in the final quarter of the twentieth century found many different forms, not only in a reawakening of the socially and politically motivated artist, generally overlooked since the fifties, but also in the chaotic diversity of those who developed in the following decades.

182 Frank Stella (b. 1936), *Talladega Three I* from the series *Circuits*, 1982. Etching, printed in black, 66 × 51⅜ (167.7 × 130.5). Jeanne C. Thayer and John B. Turner Funds

12 Pluralism and appropriation in Europe and America

KOSUTH STATED, 'ART "LIVES" through influencing other art, not by existing as the physical residue of an artist's ideas. The reason that different artists from the past are "brought alive" again is because some aspect of their work becomes "usable" by living artists.'[36] No idea about the evolution of art has been more specific to developments in the 1980s than this. The recapitulation of past styles became more than a selected use in this period when 'appropriation' became the term most descriptive of what was being done. Pluralism, the inevitable result of an information-saturated society, was now the pertinent mode of art, that is, no style prevailing over others. For some this signified the end of modernism and the beginning of post-modernism. From this time forward there would be no more discoveries, only borrowings. In fact, the first years of the eighties saw several events that seemed to indicate that the major monuments of printmaking in the years after World War II had already been created. Exhibitions in New York and Berlin covered much of the same material, announcing the new expressionist artists, the first to refer so directly to earlier movements. What choices the artists of the penultimate decade of the twentieth century had were sufficiently limited to lead to several manifestations of consciously 'bad' art, centered generally around anti-social behavior, such as the deface-ment of public property. The graffiti 'artists' obtained considerable prominence as they, together with publicized criminals, became popular rallying points for those who sought the true meaning of contemporary culture. In America, artists such as Keith Haring and Jean Michel Basquiat, who had covered subway cars and other publicly visible surfaces with their works, were popular enough to encourage publishers to have them make prints. In addition, Basquiat for a time collaborated on works with Andy Warhol. In Europe, however, only a few artists of this sort have been given equivalent attention.

Among the older artists who continued to create prints in the 1980s, such as Frank Stella and Jasper Johns, significant changes that revealed indebtedness to specific works by other artists occurred. Stella took the tools of the drafting table and scraps from stamping plates (made to produce embossed plastic tablecloths) and produced wall sculptures and prints that inaugurated what began to be referred to as neo-geo(metric) art. Johns, on the other hand, began to compose works that were more closely related to American trompe l'œil painting, organized around his own earlier imagery and objects that referred to various other illusions in art. In some cases, such as the aquatint *Spring* of 1987, he borrowed from two Picasso compositions to bring together these illusory elements (shadows and figures that may be read two ways, each mutually exclusive).

It was inevitable that a reaction to the proliferation of intellectual, dehumanized, systemic art would follow. One area of Conceptual art, led by Joseph Beuys, emphasized, through his public performances in galleries and his political manifestations, the need for society to realize its relationships as individuals with each other, with the environment, and with the past. In Germany Beuys included himself as part of his work and attracted many students and followers who found inspiration in his ritualistic, subjective approach (his personal past was evoked in such works as those in which animal fat, a dead hare, blood and honey recalled his survival from a plane crash in World War II). He created dozens of multiple art works, including prints that incorporated the symbolism of his art actions.

183 Jasper Johns (b. 1930), *Spring* from the series *The Seasons*, 1987. Aquatint and etching, printed in color, plate: $19\frac{9}{16} \times 13\frac{1}{16}$ (49.6 × 33.1). Gift of Emily Fisher Landau

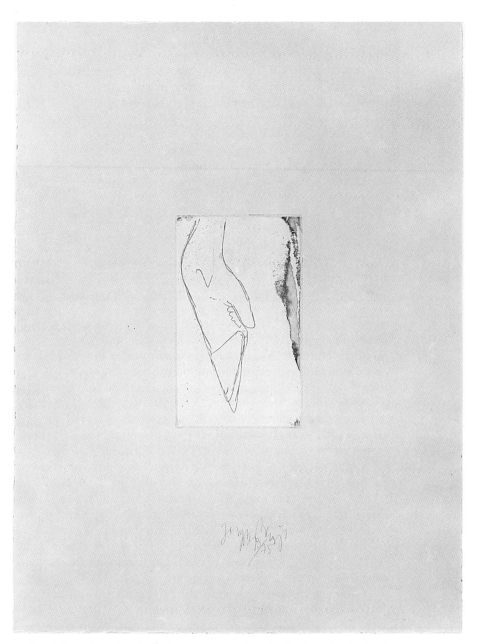

184 Joseph Beuys (1921–86). *Stag's Foot* from *Tears Suite*, 1985. Etching, printed in black, plate: $6 \times 3\frac{5}{8}$ (15.2 × 9.1). Walter Bareiss Fund

Also of considerable impact in Germany was the persistent collecting of foreign art, particularly American Pop and Minimal art, by successful businessmen and the numerous public museums. A large number of artists, reacting to these influences as well as to the unique political situation of the two Germanys, felt compelled to produce a new, expressionistic art, nearly all of it representational to some degree, with a strongly symbolic current running through it. In the German tradition, most of the major artists of this tendency have made prints. Georg Baselitz began to produce etchings and woodcuts in a figurative style reminiscent of Dubuffet in the 1960s. Soon afterwards he began to break up his figures and finally reversed them

186 entirely into an upside-down position, alluding to the inherent disorientation of the German culture. Baselitz started to cut very large linoleum and plywood sheets in 1976, producing the first of many oversized prints which revealed radical changes in attitude towards the presentation and collection of prints.

Other artists in Germany and Switzerland emerged as energetic printmakers, but none more so than Anselm Kiefer. A student of Joseph Beuys, he filled his paintings of the 1970s with collages of woodcuts or added some paint to his larger prints. He melded the techniques; there were no uniform editions of his prints, only varying

185 Anselm Kiefer (b. 1945), Page 19 from *Der Rhein*, 1983. Woodcut, printed in black, page: 23¼ × 16⅝ (59.1 × 42.2). Purchase

186 A. R. Penck (Ralf Winkler, b. 1939), *Nightvision* from the portfolio *First Concentration I*, 1982. Woodcut, printed in black, 35⅜ × 27⁵⁄₁₆ (89.8 × 69.3). Gift of Nelson Blitz, Jr

organizations of his woodblock-printed sheets. The book, *Der Rhein*, which he printed ten times, includes woodcuts which appear in other formats and often in conjunction with those that depict other subjects. Kiefer used print as a context for his paintings which, for the most part, evoke the Germanic myths of a heroic past. He is very partial to the book form as a means of conveying a process or passage in time and space through either prints or photographs that have been defaced or embellished with mud and other base materials.

Jörg Immendorf, another pupil of Beuys's, took as one of his subjects the idea of Germany as a café where all the romantic heroes and naturalistic objects met together. For several years he produced many paintings and several large prints on the subject of *Café Deutschland*. The ambitious scale of prints by the German artists referred not only to the relative sizes of their paintings but to the expansion of their influence. The printing of wood and linoleum blocks or planks did not require a press so that relief printing, besides being a traditional German technique, was also one that could be practiced in the studio.

Immendorf had developed a friendship with an East German artist who called himself A. R. Penck (Ralf Winkler), whose work was known in the West as early as the late 1960s. He moved to Cologne in

185

186

187 Susan Rothenberg (b. 1945), *Doubles*, 1980. Woodcut, printed in black, $13\frac{1}{16} \times 30\frac{7}{8}$ (33.2 × 78.5). Richard A. Epstein Fund

186 West Germany in 1980. His paintings and prints contained primitive stick figures in pictographic representations of signs and symbols that encoded a message of the commonality of all peoples and all situations from the beginning of time. This return to primitive motifs, indicators of mysterious ceremonies and instinctive beliefs that arose, as it were, from the primeval earth, recalls the early works of the American Abstract Expressionists forty years before who borrowed from ancient rock drawings of the Southwest Indians.

The earlier German expressionists also were inspired by religious objects from African tribes, but studied them for their esthetic rather than magical values. Penck, other German neo-expressionists, and several artists from Italy and America in particular, sought to transmit through the signs they chose from other cultures, their inherent capacity to communicate to the subconscious. American painters such *187* as Terry Winters and Susan Rothenberg produced prints that followed this example: Winters turning to the primitive forms of plant seeds to create heavily inked black and white lithographs made of specially developed materials that produced an effect somewhere

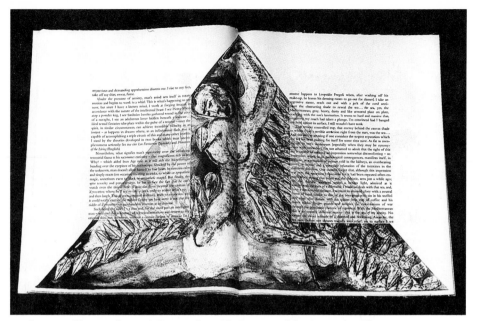

188 Francesco Clemente (b. 1952), Page 15 from *The Departure of the Argonaut* by Alberto Savinio, 1986. Lithograph, printed in color, doublepage: $25\frac{7}{8} \times 39\frac{3}{8}$ (65.7 × 100). Courtesy of Petersburg Press, Inc.

between thickly massed charcoal and dense ink; Rothenberg's woodcuts, etchings, mezzotints and lithographs depict her chosen subjects, horses which become apocalyptic, figures caught in uncontrollable action, picking out only the most essential contours to reveal not the substance but the aura of the objects.

Among the several Italian artists to emerge after the local Conceptual movement, Arte Povera, were a triumverate, Sandro Chia, Francesco Clemente and Enzio Cucchi, all of whom had considerable success in the early 1980s and also made prints. Clemente has been the most prolific printmaker, working first in etching at Crown Point Press in California, and later in New York and Italy where he produced dozens of monotypes and a monumental lithographic book, *The Departure of the Argonaut*. Clemente's work incorporates elements of the classic past of Italy, for example, the type of fresco found in his native Neapolitan area. His devotion to the Indian Hindu culture that he experiences directly each year (like many artists of this period, Clemente lives and works in more than one country) emerges in many of his images and use of color.

188

A close relationship between artists in Switzerland and Germany has existed during this century, in part because of its role as a haven during the two World Wars. The legacies of Dada and Paul Klee have manifested themselves in the works of artists as diverse as André Tomkins whose surrealist no-style works, often accomplished in Berlin, influenced German artists during his short life, and Markus Raetz, whose prints relate more to Klee in their sense of humor. Most expansive and closer to the mainstream of the neo-expressionist style, however, has been the work of Martin Disler. An example of his freely worked linoleum cuts was printed in a thirty-foot sheet and included one element that was cut, printed, then cut again and printed, thus preventing any duplication of the composition. At the time of this complex print, Disler's work shared with several of the Germans a simplified, pictographic rendering which, in his case, evolved into a wild, compulsive expressiveness that recalls the work of COBRA artist Asger Jorn in the 1950s, except that the scale of the work is that of the 1980s.

In Austria there seems to have been a consistently eccentric and extremist approach to art in the twentieth century. Performance or artist-centered work there in recent years has encompassed print-making as well. Simultaneously with the emergence of Hundert-wasser, mentioned earlier, Arnulf Rainer embarked upon his unique program of scratching on plates. His earliest prints taken from these plates date from 1964, but the same plates, progressively covered with more scratches, capturing the ink ever more thickly, were still being printed in 1986 and the artist had no intention of abandoning them. He has applied this style, which might be referred to as the obsessive defacement of surface or image (he has made both paintings and prints in which the lines cover photographs of himself and others) in several collaborations with other artists, but only with his fellow Austrian, Günter Brus, in print. In these works Brus, whose imagery is a hybrid of Austrian fantasy and neo-expressionism, drew on old copper plates that carried the remnants of botanical compositions. For his part, Rainer scratched over some of the older imagery, producing an unrecognizable but talismanic form that interacts with Brus's less aggressive but equally magical drawings.

190

This type of obsessiveness which graphically asserts the tempera-ment is manifest in the later work of the American Jim Dine who, since 1975, has exploited the random marks and flaws on his copper

191

216

189 Georg Baselitz (b. 1938), *Nude with Three Arms*, unpublished first state, April 6, 1977. Hand painted linoleum cut, printed in color, $98\frac{7}{16} \times 59\frac{13}{16}$ (250 × 152). Jeanne C. Thayer and Purchase Funds >

190 Günter Brus and Arnulf
Rainer, Plate I from the
portfolio *Depth Obscured*, 1985–
86. Etching, photoetching and
drypoint, printed in black, plate:
$17\frac{13}{16} \times 12\frac{7}{16}$ (45.2 × 31.5). Walter
Bareiss Fund

191 Jim Dine (b. 1935), *The Tree in Soot*,
1981. Etching and monotype, printed in
color, plate: $44\frac{13}{16} \times 34\frac{5}{8}$ (113.8 × 87.9).
John B. Turner Fund

192 Howard Hodgkin (b. 1932), *Two to Go*, 1981. Lithograph, printed in color with gouache additions, 36⅛ × 48¼ (91.8 × 122.6). Gift of the artist

plates. He also has drawn over his prints and heavily abraded their surfaces as he removed unwanted passages by erasing and scraping. His intaglio works from the beginning have been expressionist in character, so the work of his middle age, though often repeating the subjects of his Pop period, has a wild and unmistakably personal tone to it. His monstrous trees are as much portraits of the artist as his robe had been in the 1960s. Another artist who radically changed his style in the 1970s was the British artist Malcolm Morley. His earliest success came with painted versions of color postcards, bridging the Pop and Neorealist styles in the early 1970s. Later, interest in classical myths and various heroic or disastrous moments in literature and other media became, with a freer brushwork, the subject of both paintings and aquatints printed by a Yugoslavian, Gordan Novak, in Toronto, with such titles as *Cradles of Civilization* and *French Legionnaires being Eaten by a Lion*, of 1984.   *194*

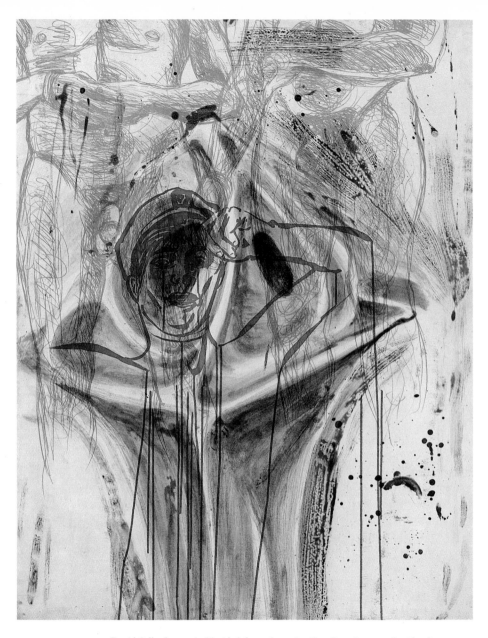

193 David Salle (b. 1952), Untitled from the series *Grandiose Synonym for Church*, 1985. Etching and aquatint, printed in color, plate: $47\frac{15}{16} \times 37\frac{3}{4}$ (121.7 × 95.8). John B. Turner Fund

194 Malcolm Morley (b. 1931), *French Legionnaires being Eaten by a Lion*, 1984. Etching and aquatint, printed in color, plate: $20\frac{11}{16} \times 32\frac{15}{16}$ (52.6 × 83.6). Dorothy Braude Edinburg Fund

The paintings and prints of another British artist, Howard *192*
Hodgkin, have indicated that a kind of abstraction from nature which
yet conveys a place and atmosphere is a sensible formula for late
twentieth-century art. In prints, often larger in scale than his paintings
and occasionally printed in two versions, color as well as black and
white, Hodgkin presents framed scenes in which the specific objects
are made up of organized, simplified forms that allude to the subject
rather than describe it.

In America two artists closely associated with the more expressionist (or less categorizably structured) compositional styles, Julian
Schnabel and David Salle, were both invited to make prints by Parasol
Press, which had been the foremost publisher of the minimalist artists.
Schnabel, whose paintings were upon broken plates and discarded
theatrical scenery, was intrigued by the possibilities of printing upon
equally unusual materials. He created a series of prints in his obscured
figurative style on velvet, and another on maps. Salle, whose style was *195*
basically a layering of familiar imagery, from Walt Disney to Oscar *193*
Kokoschka, made several series of prints in which his drawings of

221

female figures and heads were immersed into a dense tangle of this sort of eclectic sandwich.

Among the techniques that became more acceptable during the 1980s was the addition of handcoloring, either directly on the printing form or on the print itself. Monotype, essentially a handpainted composition made on a plate that prints only once in the brightness of the original painting but is often reprinted several times, became a popular technique after an exhibition devoted to its history in New York in 1980. However, in most countries there have been artists who were less interested in the repeatability of the print media than in the unique look printed surfaces have. Thus, while Johns, Clemente, Dine and many others made pure monotypes, they also enhanced previously printed compositions with monotype. In Europe, Immendorf and Baselitz painted over their woodcuts, and Kiefer's prints are always altered in this way. It seems that these and many other artists have sought to expand the creative parameters of the print. This may be a manifestation of freedom from the mechanical restrictions of the edition print, but the reason seems more likely to be the artist's more intense involvement with the medium. One surmises that had the Abstract Expressionists had the large presses and large sheets of paper that were developed by the late 1970s, they too would have managed to make prints, and more than likely those prints would have been either monotypes or paint-enhanced prints. The development, however, of such materials could only occur after a period of work during which artists realized the possibilities inherent in the media, could work with printers to develop new materials and insist on having the flexibility to work with and on them.

To follow the widespread activities of artists, print workshops have opened and publishers have encouraged printmaking activity in many areas of the world. For example, in Berlin a screenprinting workshop has worked intensively with local artists such as Rainer Fetting, Helmut Middendorf, and the frequently visiting Scottish performance artist and painter, Bruce McLean. In France a young lithography printer worked first in Lyon and then in Paris with such visiting artists as the theatrical designer and author, Robert Wilson, as well as with French and German artists. In Germany the Munich publisher Sabine Knust, working at first with Heiner Friedrich to produce the works of Palermo, Richter and others in the 1970s, has continued by producing the first groups of prints to document the neo-expressionists, *Erste*

195 Julian Schnabel (b. 1951), *Brenda*, 1984. Aquatint, printed in black on velvet, $59\frac{7}{8} \times 35\frac{7}{8}$ (152.1 × 91.2). The Associates Fund

Konzentration. Among the artists in these portfolios were Baselitz and Penck as well as the Danish artist, Per Kirkeby, whose career was closely connected with the neo-expressionists from Germany. Another publisher, working mainly in Switzerland, Peter Blum, has produced portfolios of work by the Italians Sandro Chia and Clemente, as well as prints by several Americans who emerged in the 1980s, specifically Eric Fischl and Jonathan Borofsky. Large-scale aquatints by Fischl, Cucchi and Mimmo Paladino, met the requirements of those who collected prints as realistic equivalents to the overscaled paintings and sculptures of these artists.

In this discussion much has been left out about the emergence of great numbers of women artists in America who have had the opportunities as few of their predecessors had of making prints with the most prominent printers and publishers. Elsewhere, the proliferation of prints made for competitions in countries of the Far East and Eastern Europe did not diminish. However, these prints oddly never found as vast an international audience as before, despite the magnitude of the artistic population and economic interests in promoting art that occurred in the European community and in America. Given the lengthy period of relative peace, and the great possibilities of nearly unimpeded travel, the diminution of substantive creativity in the West is obviously a product of some other combination of circumstances. One thinks of the 1880s and the rise of post-impressionism, the artists of which actually created the formulae for twentieth-century art. With the desperate search that has been undertaken among Western artists, rapidly followed by that of the Japanese, certainly the quantity of styles, forms and ambitions should have produced some equivalent discovery and formulation in the eighties of this century. Perhaps the close ties prints have with economic trends make the appearance of the new less noticeable, since only the few artists who have enough of an economic base (that is, purchasers for their product) will have the opportunity to make prints. This is not to say that in the communities of young artists there are not a few who, as the Germans did, make prints on the floors of their workrooms and studios. There are, too, those whose economics are sufficient for them to experiment with electronics, printing out graphics on their computers. Why, so far, no mention has been made of this new technology, seems to be a curious situation, for artists all over the world, particularly in schools and in businesses, have had access to this technology for well over two decades. Recall, however, that lithography was developed at the end of the eighteenth century, and while it was used to document scenes and events, it found few artists capable of creating with it until the end of the nineteenth century. What is the purpose of the pictures of our time if not to allow the imagination the free rein that so much documentation in the form of numbers, letters, patterns on video and computer screens, constricts.

IN CONCLUDING THIS HISTORY of twentieth-century art as viewed through the prints created during this period, the author offers an apology to those who may not have found herein a discussion of their favorite printmakers, and to those who incredulously question the inclusion of so many artists of the last quarter-century who seem to be of less consequence. Regrettably, few historians have access to a crystal ball revealing events that will intensify the meanings of some occurrences and obliterate others. Should the reader feel that the chosen examples have faded, there nevertheless remains evidence that those prints reflected specific concerns shared by many artists creating in similar circumstances. One finds, again, that no works by artists of the past are viewed in the same manner now as they were at the time of their first exposure. While the writings of critics contemporaneous with many of the works have been cited, the quotations selected here have inevitably been the ones that most closely agree with the opinions of our time. Within the last two decades the Conceptual artists reduced visual art to unembellished ideas and others have had their short-lived styles prefixed with Neo-. Once more, the hopscotch progress of art means it is nearly impossible to make predictions.

At this point in the twentieth century we have looked back upon more than eight decades of unequaled effort and production in the field of printmaking. The period produced in Picasso an undisputed genius, whose devotion to art resulted in a vast printed *œuvre* astonishingly rich in its imagery. The proliferation of prints followed the expansion of European esthetic ideas into the entire world. After World War II and the development of rapid and massive communication, art became a recognized part of the exchange of ideas. The directors of enlarged exhibition facilities took advantage of the comparatively safe and swift transportation offered by the airplane between distant nations to show works of art previously familiar only through reproductions, while periodicals and television repeated and dispersed names and images. The subsequent widespread interest in the acquisition of original works – for most people financially possible only in the area of prints – led to the expansion of commercial enterprises devoted to art. This expansion, as has been seen, also included new facilities to produce prints. Numerous print publishers and print-collecting organizations were established during these years, and ultimately the print buyer's need to be protected from fraudulent practices became an overly important part of print connoisseurship. Because of competition among collectors and the unfortunate categorization of some prints as excellent objects for investment, the monetary value of prints has often exceeded that of unique works of similar quality.

The rapidity with which the visual arts have been transformed in recent years is all too apparent. The last few decades of prosperity and relatively low manslaughter in the industrialized areas of the world have seen a disproportionate increase in persons pursuing careers in the fine arts. Exploration and experimentation by those artists whose upbringing was largely 'permissive' and whose education was similarly undisciplined have led to a proliferation of ideas of questionable value. While society is still financially and psychologically able to tolerate this excess of artistic production of uneven quality, it is quite possible that this most recent decade in our century is one of drain rather than progress. Each period has its detractors, and one can cite critics who have doomsdayed each new development in art. The *tabula rasa* efforts of the Conceptualists were a backboard for the rebound of creative efforts that sought from the past a way to the future. With changing social conditions, the contrived commercial manipulation of the artist's work in the print media may diminish, precipitating the artist into a different relationship with the market and with the opportunity to create. This does not necessarily mean, as some printmakers would have it, simply a return to hand-cranking a press and producing small editions. It does imply the freedom to work with any means and materials that the artist desires, printing only those images with which the artist is completely satisfied in editions that reflect all the possibilities and limitations of the chosen medium. Prints are, indeed, a commodity exactly because they are not unique. The decision to make them more precious by artificially limiting each edition is in direct opposition to the historical development of the print and printing itself. At this moment when prints have become plentiful but often dubious objects of cultural commitment, few would question their importance in the history of twentieth-century art. Only the future will show which works of our time contain the seeds that will nurture its own art.

Notes on the text

1 Matisse, Henri, 'Notes d'un peintre,' *La Grande Revue* (Paris, 25 December 1908) pp. 731–45, trans. in Alfred H. Barr, Jr., *Matisse: His Art and His Public* (New York, The Museum of Modern Art, 1951)

2 Translation in *Voices of German Expressionism*, ed. Victor H. Meisel (Englewood Cliffs, N.J., Prentice-Hall, 1970)

3 Louis de Marsalle (pseud. E.L. Kirchner), 'Uber Kirchners Graphik,' *Genius* (Munich, 1921) pp. 250–63

4 Ernst Barlach, letter to Reinhard Piper, 28 December 1911, trans. in *Voices of German Expressionism*, ed. Victor H. Meisel (Englewood Cliffs, N.J., Prentice-Hall, 1970)

5 Letter from Cézanne to Emile Bernard, 15 April 1904, published *Mercure de France*, 16 October 1907, pp. 617–18.

6 *Gil Blas* (14 November 1908), trans. in Herschel B. Chipp, *Theories of Modern Art* (University of California Press, 1970) pp. 206f.

7 And the General [M.P. Dagog] received this note with surprise: Make haste! Buy Royal Dutch! Sell Petits Beurre.
'Ah! What confusion! Ah! What confusion!' sang out the General, hands behind his back,
'I resign myself to this confusion!' said the cunning *tourtelette*.
Translator's note: We do not know if it is little tart (tourtelette), tartlet (tartelette) or letter-card (cartelettre); the papyrus characters have suffered the injuries of time.

8 Gropius, Walter, *Idee und Aufbau des Staatlichen Bauhauses Weimar* (Weimar, Bauhausverlag, 1923), trans. in *Bauhaus 1919–1928*, ed. H. Bayer, W. & I. Gropius (New York, The Museum of Modern Art, 1938) p. 20

9 Huelsenbeck, Richard, *Avant Dada: Eine Geschichte des Dadaismus* (Hanover, Stelgemann, 1920), trans. by Ralph Manheim, *The Dada Painters and Poets: An Anthology*, ed. Robert Motherwell (New York, Wittenborn, Schultz, 1951)

10 *Der Ararat* (Munich), vol. 2, No. 1, 1921, pp. 5–6, trans. by Ralph Manheim, *The Dada Painters and Poets*, pp. 59–60

11 Breton, André, *Manifeste du Surréalisme* (Paris, 1924), trans. in William S. Rubin, *Dada, Surrealism, and Their Heritage* (New York, The Museum of Modern Art, 1968) p. 64

12 Ernst, Max, 'Au delà de la Peinture,' *Cahiers d'Art* (Paris), XI, 6–7, 1936, trans. by Dorothea Tanning in Max Ernst, *Beyond Painting* (New York, Wittenborn, Schultz, 1948)

13 Ernst's small etching for the cover of *Au 125 du boulevard Saint-Germain* by Benjamin Péret (Paris, Collection Littérature, 1923) is also a candidate for this honor.

14 Breton, André, *ibid.*

15 Sweeney, J.J., 'Joan Miró, Comment and Interview,' *Partisan Review*, No. 2, February 1948, p. 212

16 Breton, A., *Le Surréalisme et la Peinture* (New York, Brentano's, 1945) p. 68

17 Dali, Salvador, 'Philosophical Provocations' in *Documents 34* (Brussels, 15 May 1934), quoted in André Breton, *Qu'est-ce-que le Surréalisme?* (Brussels, R. Henriquez, 1934)

18 Soby, James Thrall, *Salvador Dali* (New York, The Museum of Modern Art, 1946) p. 14

19 Calas, Nicolas, 'Saper Vedere' in *Brunidor Portfolio Number One* (New York, Brunidor Editions, 1947)

20 Matisse, 'Comment je fais mes livres,' *Anthologie du livre illustré*, ed. Albert Skira, 1944, trans. in William S. Lieberman, *Matisse, 50 Years of his Graphic Art* (New York, Braziller, 1956) p.12

21 Matisse, Henri, *Jazz* (Paris, Tériade, 1947) pp. 141–42

22 Howe, Russell W., 'Chalk and Cheese: Puy and Léger,' *Apollo* (London), vol. 50, August 1949, pp. 31–3

23 Léger, Fernand, *Cirque* (Paris, Tériade, 1950) p. 51

24 Davis, Stuart, quoted in Sam Hunter, *Modern American Painting and Sculpture* (New York, Laurel, 1959) p. 128

25 Breton, André, 'Le Surréalisme et la Peinture,' *La Révolution Surréaliste*, No. 4, Paris, 15 July 1925

26 Hopper, Edward, 'John Sloan and the Philadelphians,' *The Arts,* April 1927, vol. XI, No. 4, p. 174

27 In 1938 the Graphic Arts Division of the Works Progress Administration had a silkscreen workshop in New York under the direction of Anthony Velonis. In 1940 several artists working there formed the Silk Screen Group, which became the National Serigraph Society in 1944.

28 James Lang, review of McMillen, Inc., New York exhibition, *Art News*, 15 January 1942, p. 31

29 Giacometti, Alberto, 'Le rêve, le sphinx et la mort de T.,' *Labyrinthe* (Paris), No. 22, December 1946, p. 12

30 Escher, M.C., *The Graphic Work of M.C. Escher* (New York, Ballantine, 1971)

31 Letter to Alison and Peter Smithson, 16 January 1957, quoted in *Richard Hamilton*, introduction by Richard Morphet (London, Tate Gallery, 1970)

32 Swenson, Gene R., 'What Is Pop Art?,' interview with Roy Lichtenstein, *Art News*, vol. 62 No. 7, November 1963, pp. 25, 62

33 Staber, Margit, *Max Bill* (New York, Fernhill, 1964) p. 23

34 Kosuth, Joseph, 'Art After Philosophy, I & II,' *Studio International*, October and November 1969, reprinted in *Idea Art*, ed. G. Battcock (New York, Dutton, 1973) p. 93

35 Sarah Charlesworth, 'A Declaration of Independence,' *The Fox*, Spring, 1975, p. 1

36 Kosuth, Joseph, *ibid.*, p. 82

Glossary of printmaking terms

Aquatint: An intaglio print taken from a metal plate which has been etched through a porous ground of powdered and melted resin so as to produce a fine-textured effect of ink wash when printed.

Drypoint: An intaglio print taken from a metal plate into which the lines forming the image are scratched with a metal or crystal point. The tool leaves a residue of metal along the edges which will capture some ink, giving a distinctive furry line.

Engraving: An intaglio print taken from a metal plate into which the lines forming the image are cut with a wedge-shaped tool called a 'burin.'

Etching: An intaglio print taken from a metal plate into which the image has been bitten with acid. Lines may be scratched through a layer of varnish or other impervious material (hard ground), or pressed into a nonhardening impervious material (soft ground), or drawn with a water-soluble substance that is allowed to dry, covered with an impervious material, and then soaked in water so that the material over the drawing lifts (lift-ground or sugar-lift). An acid bath of variable composition and duration etches away all areas where the ground is removed and the plate exposed, creating grooves and textures that will hold ink.

Intaglio technique: Grooves and other altered areas below the surface of a metal plate form or control the image. Copper and zinc are the usual materials for the plates. Ink introduced into the grooves and cleaned from the original surface of the plate will print when plate and dampened paper are run through a press under extreme pressure. Normally the plate is smaller than the paper and its impression remains on the paper. See *Aquatint, Drypoint, Engraving, Etching,* and *Mezzotint.*

Linoleum cut (lino-cut): A relief print made from a block of linoleum cut in the same manner as a woodcut. The printed surface has less texture than in a woodcut because of the homogeneous nature of linoleum.

Lithograph: A planographic print made from a special type of stone (Bavarian limestone), metal plate (zinc, aluminum or other), or coated paper, all of which retain grease and reject water. The image is created directly upon the stone or plate with greasy pencil, crayon and/or liquid (*tusche*) or else transferred from treated paper. After a series of treatments alternating light etching and inking, the stone or plate is dampened and rolled with ink, which will remain only in areas where the image has been drawn.

Mezzotint: An intaglio print from a metal plate which has been manually scratched or pitted with a rocker (a multitoothed tool). The pits are subsequently smoothed away to form areas that will no longer hold ink.

Monotype: A single printing of an image incapable of being identically reprinted. The most common technique is painting the image on glass or metal and printing before the ink or paint dries.

Photomechanical techniques: The image is transferred by means of light passing through a photographic negative onto a light-sensitized printing surface. In order to obtain grays in relief, intaglio, and stencil techniques, a fine screen must be introduced to break up the image into areas of varying densities.

Planographic technique: The image to be printed is created upon the surface of a stone or plate which is altered chemically rather than dimensionally. The stone or plate is inked, covered with paper, and printed on a flat-bed press. Plates made in this manner may also be printed on an offset press. See *Lithograph.*

Relief technique: The image is printed from the portion of a block of rigid material that remains above cut-out areas or from materials added to a flat surface. Relief prints other than woodcut and linoleum cut utilize cut pieces of cardboard or paper pasted in a low-relief image, plastic glue hardened into shapes, cast objects, and other forms of relief. Printing is done either by rubbing the verso of paper placed on the inked surface of the block or by running the

paper and block through a press. See *Linoleum cut* and *Woodcut.*

Serigraph: See *Silkscreen.*

Silkscreen: A print made by passing ink or paint through a screen of cloth, usually silk but more recently synthetic material, to which a stencil has been adhered. The stencil may be made of adhesive film, cut or prepared photographically, or may be a brushed-on coating, often applied over an image made with water-soluble material, which allows the coating over it to be washed away.

Stencil technique: The image is created from open space in a cut or shaped form which will allow ink or paint to pass through when applied with a brush (*pochoir*), airbrush, or squeegee (silkscreen). See *Silkscreen.*

Woodcut: A relief print made from a plank of wood (usually cut on the straight grain) from which areas meant to remain uninked are cut away with a gouge or sharp knife.

Bibliography

General Reference

C. Adams *American Lithographs, 1900–1960: Artists and Their Prints.* Albuquerque, University of New Mexico Press, 1983
American Prints 1960–1985 in the Collection of the Museum of Modern Art. New York, Museum of Modern Art, 1986
G. Z. Antreasian and C. Adams *The Tamarind Book of Lithography: Art and Techniques.* New York, Abrams, 1971
Ars Multiplicata. Vervielfältigte Kunst seit 1945. Cologne, Wallraf-Richartz Museum, 1968

Amerikanische und Englische Graphik der Gegenwart. Stuttgart, Staatsgalerie, 1974
K. Beall *American Prints in the Library of Congress.* Baltimore, Johns Hopkins University Press, [1970]
E. M. Bloch *Words and Images: Universal Limited Art Editions.* Los Angeles, University of California at Los Angeles Art Council, 1978
R. Block *Grafik des Kapitalistischen Realismus.* Berlin, René Block, 1971
F. Brunner *A Handbook of Graphic Reproduction Processes.* New York, Hastings, 1962

L.-G. Buchheim *The Graphic Art of German Expressionism*. New York, Universe Books, 1960

R. Castleman *Technics and Creativity: Gemini G.E.L.* New York, Museum of Modern Art, 1971

R. Castleman *Contemporary Prints*. New York, Viking, 1973

R. Castleman *Modern Art in Prints*. New York, Museum of Modern Art, 1973

R. Castleman *Latin American Prints from The Museum of Modern Art*. New York, Center for Inter-American Relations, 1974

R. Castleman *Printed Art: A View of Two Decades*. New York, Museum of Modern Art, 1980

R. Castleman *American Impressions: Prints since Pollock*. New York, Knopf, 1986

J. Coolidge *Master Prints of the Twentieth Century*. Cambridge, Harvard University Press, 1965

A. Dückers *Druckgraphik Wandlungen eines Mediums seit 1945*. Berlin, Staatliches Museen Preussischer Kulturbesitz, 1981

R. Field *Offset Lithography*. Middletown, Davison Art Center, 1973

R. Field *Recent American Etching*. Washington, D.C., National Collection of Fine Arts, Smithsonian Institution, 1975

R. Fine *Gemini G. E. L.: Art and Collaboration*. Washington, D.C., National Gallery of Art; New York, Abbeville Press, 1984

M. Friedman *et al. Tyler Graphics: The Extended Image.* Minneapolis, Walker Art Center; New York, Abbeville Press, 1987

E. M. Garvey *The Artist and the Book 1860–1960*, P. Hofer, intro. Boston, Museum of Fine Arts, [1961]

F. and D. Getlein *The Bite of the Print*. New York, Potter, 1963

P. Gilmour *Modern Prints*. New York, Studio Vista/Dutton, 1970

P. Gilmour *The Mechanized Image*. London, Arts Council of Great Britain, 1978

P. Gilmour and A. Wellsford *Paperwork*. Canberra, Australian National Gallery, 1982

J. Goldman *American Prints, Process and Proofs*. New York, Whitney Museum of American Art/Harper and Row, 1981

Grafische Techniken. Berlin, Neuen Berliner Kunstvereins, 1973

S. W. Hayter *About Prints*. London, Oxford University Press, 1962

J. Heller *Printmaking Today*. New York, Holt, Rinehart and Winston, 1972

C. Hogben and R. Watson, eds. *From Manet to Hockney: Modern Artists' Illustrated Books*. London, Victoria and Albert Museum, 1985

Das Informel in der Europäischen Druckgraphik Sammlung Prelinger. Munich, Staatliche Graphische Sammlung, 1985

C. Ives *The Painterly Print*. New York, Metropolitan Museum of Art, 1980

W. Ivins, Jr. *Notes on Prints*. New York, Da Capo Press, 1967

E. L. Johnson *Contemporary Painters and Sculptors as Printmakers*. New York, Museum of Modern Art, 1966

D. Koepplin *Kubismus. Zeichnung and Druckgraphik*. Basel, Kunstmuseum, 1968

F. H. Man *Artist's Lithographs*. New York, Putnam's, 1969

R. Passeron *French Prints of the 20th Century*. New York, Praeger, 1970

H. Platt *Artist's Prints in Colour*. London, Barrie and Rockliff, 1961

P. J. Sachs *Modern Prints and Drawings*. New York, Knopf, 1954

K. Sotriffer *Expressionismus und Fauvismus*. Vienna and Munich, A. Schroll, 1971

O. Statler *Modern Japanese Prints*. Rutland, Vt., Tuttle, 1956

W. Stubbe *Graphic Arts in the Twentieth Century*. New York/London, Praeger, 1963

K. E. Tyler *Tyler Graphics: Catalogue Raisonné 1974–1985.* Minneapolis, Walker Art Center; New York, Abbeville Press, 1987

J. Watrous *A Century of American Printmaking, 1880–1980.* Madison, University of Wisconsin Press, 1984

W. Weber *A History of Lithography.* New York, McGraw-Hill; London, Thames and Hudson, 1966

P. Wember *Blattkunste Internationale Druckgraphik seit 1945.* Krefeld, Kaiser Wilhelm Museum/Scherpe Verlag, 1973

C. Zigrosser *The Book of Fine Prints.* New York, Crown, 1956

C. Zigrosser *The Expressionists: A Survey of Their Graphic Art.* New York, Braziller, 1957

C. Zigrosser *The Appeal of Prints.* Philadelphia, Leary's Co., 1970

MONOGRAPHS

Josef Albers at the Metropolitan Museum of Art. New York, Metropolitan Museum of Art, 1971

J. Miller *Josef Albers: Prints 1915–1970.* Brooklyn, The Brooklyn Museum, 1973

Pierre Alechinsky Les Estampes de 1946 á 1972. Paris, Yves Rivière, 1973

G. Gercken *Werkverzeichnis des Radierungen Horst Antes 1962–66.* Munich, Galerie Stangl, 1968

Arakawa: Print Works, 1965–1979. Kitakyushu, Kitakyushu City Museum of Art, 1979

D. Karshan *Archipenko The Sculpture and Graphic Art.* Tübingen, Wasmuth, 1974

Arp Graphik 1912–1959. Bern, Kornfeld and Klipstein, 1959.

W. F. Arntz, ed. *Arntz-Bulletin, Dokumentation der Kunst des Zwanzigsten Jahrhunderts,* 'Hans Arp – Graphik,' vol. 1, Nos. 3–11 (1969–74)

J. Petit *Baj, catalogue de l'œuvre graphique et des multiples,* vols. i–ii. Geneva, Rousseau, [1971], 1973

J. Petit *Baj, catalogue de l'œuvre gravé et lithographié 1952–1970.* n.p., n.d.

F. Schult *Ernst Barlach Das graphische Werk,* Hamburg, Hauswedell, 1958

F. Jahn *Baselitz, Werkverzeichnis der Druckgrafik 1963–1974,* vol. i. Bern/Berlin, Verlag Gachnang und Springer, 1983

Leonard Baskin: The Graphic Work 1950–70. New York, FAR Gallery, 1970

A. Fern and J. O'Sullivan *The Complete Prints of Leonard Baskin: A Catalogue Raisonné 1948–1983.* Boston, Little, Brown, 1984

K. Gallwitz *Max Beckmann. Die Druckgraphik 1910–1948.* Karlsruhe, Badischer Kunstverein, 1962

A. Pieyre de Mandiargues *Hans Bellmer, Œuvre gravé.* Paris, Denoël, 1969

C. Fath *The Lithographs of Thomas Hart Benton.* Austin, University of Texas Press, 1969

Joseph Beuys Multiples: Catalogue Raisonné of Multiples and Prints 1965–1985. Munich/New York, Edition Schellmann, 1985

J. Floury in C. Terrasse, *Bonnard.* Paris, Floury, 1927

C. Roger-Marx *Bonnard, Lithographie.* Monte Carlo, Sauret, 1952

F. Mourlot *Braque Lithographe, Catalogue Complet.* Monte Carlo, Sauret, 1963

E. Engelberts and H. Wünsche *Georges Braque. Das lithographische Werk.* Bonn, Wünsche, 1971

D. Vallier *Braque L'Œuvre gravé.* Paris, Flammarion, 1982

Marcel Broodthaers, Editionen 1964–1975. Munich, Galerie Heiner Friedrich, 1978

F. Meyer *Marc Chagall, Das Graphische Werk.* Stuttgart, Hatje, 1957

F. Mourlot and C. Sorlier *Chagall Lithographe,* vols. i–iv. Monte Carlo, Sauret, 1960–74

J. Adhémar *Chagall l'œuvre gravé.* Paris, Bibliothèque Nationale, 1970

E. W. Kornfeld *Verzeichnis der Kupfer-*

stiche Radierungen und Holzschnitte von Marc Chagall. 1922–66, vol. i. Bern, Kornfeld and Klipstein, 1970

K. Schwarz Das graphische Werk von Lovis Corinth. Berlin, Gurlitt, 1922

H. Mueller Die späte Graphik von Lovis Corinth. Hamburg, Lichtwarkstiftung, 1960

Pierre Courtin L'Œuvre gravé, 1944–1972. Paris, Yves Rivière, 1973

J. Myers, ed. Stuart Davis: Graphic Work and Related Paintings. Fort Worth, Amon Carter Museum, 1986

J. Loyer and C. Perussaux, 'Robert Delaunay Catalogue de son œuvre lithographique' in Nouvelles de l'estampe, No. 15 (1974)

Jim Dine Complete Graphics. Berlin, Galerie Mikro, 1970

T. Krens Jim Dine Prints: 1970–1977. New York, Harper and Row in association with the Williams College Artist-in-Residence Program, 1977

E. D'Oench and J. Feinberg Jim Dine: Prints 1977–1985. New York, Harper and Row, 1986

F. Karsch Otto Dix Das graphische Werk. Hanover, Fackelträger-Verlag Schmidt Küster GmbH, 1970

N. Arnaud Jean Dubuffet, gravures et lithographies. Silkeborg, Silkeborg Museum, 1961

U. Schmitt Supplément au catalogue des gravures et lithographies de Jean Dubuffet. Paris, C. Bernart, 1966

M. Loreau Catalogue des Travaux de Jean Dubuffet, vol. xvi, 'Les Phénomènes.' Paris, J.-J. Pauvert, 1964

P. Courthion Raoul Dufy. Geneva, Cailler, 1951

Hugues & Poupard-Lieussou M. Ernst, Ecrits et Œuvre gravé. Paris, Le Point Cardinal, 1963

W. Spies and H. R. Leppien Max Ernst, Das graphische Werk. Houston, Menil Fdn., and Cologne, Dumont Schauberg, 1975

J. L. Locher, ed. The World of M. C. Escher. New York, Abrams, [1971]

L. Prasse Lyonel Feininger. A Definitive Catalogue of his Graphic Work: Etchings, Lithographs, Woodcuts. Cleveland, Museum of Art, [1972]

Sam Francis Werke, 1960–1. Bern, Kornfeld and Klipstein, 1961

T. Krens Helen Frankenthaler: Prints 1961–1979. New York, Harper and Row, 1979

Antonio Frasconi Against the Grain, N. Hentoff, intro. New York, Macmillan, 1974

H. Weis Ernst Fuchs, Das graphische Werk. Munich, Ketterer, 1967

C. Lust Giacometti, The Complete Graphics. New York, Tudor, 1970

D.-H. Kahnweiler Gris His Life and Work. New York, Abrams, [1969]

R. Field The Prints of Richard Hamilton. Middletown, Davison Art Center, 1973

Richard Hamilton Prints: A Complete Catalogue of Graphic Works 1939–1983. Stuttgart, Hansjörg Meyer; London, Waddington Graphics, 1984

R. Schmücking Hans Hartung, Werkverzeichnis der Graphik 1921–65. Brunswick, Schmücking, 1965

S. W. Hayter New Ways of Gravure. New York, Pantheon, 1949

G. Reynolds The Engravings of S. W. Hayter. London, Victoria and Albert Museum, 1967

A. and W.-D. Dube Erich Heckel Das graphische Werk, vols. i–iii. New York, Rathenau, 1964, 1965, 1974

Anton Heyboer, J. L. Lochner, intro. The Hague, Eindhoven, Amsterdam, 1967–68

M. Glasebrook David Hockney . . . 1960–70. London, Whitechapel Art Gallery, 1970

G. Baro David Hockney: Prints and Drawings. Washington, D.C., International Exhibitions Foundation, 1978

Howard Hodgkin: Prints 1977–1983.

London, Tate Gallery, 1985

'The Etchings of Edward Hopper' in C. Zigrosser, *Prints*. New York, Holt, Rinehart and Winston, 1962

W. Koschatzky *Friedensreich Hundertwasser: The Complete Graphic Work 1951–1986*. New York, Rizzoli, 1986

J. Nichiwaki *et al. Masuo Ikeda – Graphic Works 1956–71*. Tokyo, Bijutsu Shuppan-sha, 1972

W. Katz *Robert Indiana: The Prints and Posters 1961–1971*. Stuttgart/New York, Edition Domberger, 1971

W. Schmied *Horst Janssen*. Hanover, Kestner-Gesellschaft, 1966

R. Field *Jasper Johns: Prints 1960–70*. Philadelphia, Museum of Art, 1970

C. Huber *Jasper Johns Graphik*. Bern, Kornfeld and Klipstein, 1971

R. Field *Jasper Johns: Prints 1970–1977*. Middletown, Wesleyan University Press, 1978

R. Castleman *Jasper Johns: A Print Retrospective*. New York, Museum of Modern Art, 1986

H. K. Röthel *Kandinsky Das graphische Werk*. Cologne, Dumont Schauberg, [1970]

D. Waldman *Ellsworth Kelly, Drawings, Collages, Prints*. Greenwich Conn., New York Graphic Society, [1971]

R. H. Axsom *The Prints of Ellsworth Kelly*. New York, Hudson Hills Press, 1987

A. and W.-D. Dube. *E. L. Kirchner. Das graphische Werk*, vols. i–ii. Munich, Prestel, 1967

R. B. Kitaj *Complete Graphics 1964–69*. Berlin, Galerie Mikro, 1969

E. W. Kornfeld *Paul Klee*. Bern, Kornfeld and Klipstein, 1963

H. W. Singer *Max Klingers Radierungen, Stiche und Steindrucke*. Berlin, Amster und Ruthardt, 1909

W. F. Arntz, 'Das graphische Werk Kokoschkas' in *Oskar Kokoschka Ausstellung*. Munich, Prestel, 1950

A. Klipstein *Käthe Kollwitz. The Graphic Work*. New York, St. Etienne, 1955

J. Ashbery, 'Willem de Kooning,' *Art News Annual*, New York, 1971

C. Zigrosser *Mauricio Lasansky*. New York, American Federation of Arts, 1960

Henri Laurens, Exposition de la donation aux Musées Nationaux. Paris, Grand Palais, 1967

L. Saphire *Fernand Léger: The Complete Graphic Work*. New York, Blue Moon Press, 1978

E. Petermann *Die Druckgraphik von Wilhelm Lehmbruck*. Stuttgart, Hatje, 1964

Sol LeWitt, Graphik 1970–1975. Basel, Kunsthalle; Bern, Verlag Kornfeld, 1975

Sol LeWitt: Prints 1970–86. London, Tate Gallery, 1986

D. Waldman *Roy Lichtenstein, Drawings and Prints*, New York, Chelsea House, 1972

Bernice Rose *The Drawings of Roy Lichtenstein*. New York, Museum of Modern Art, 1987

M. Guerin *Catalogue Raisonné de l'œuvre gravé de Aristide Maillol*, vols. i–ii. Geneva, P. Cailler, 1967

K. Lankheit *Franz Marc Katalog der Werke*. Cologne, Dumont Schauberg, 1970

J. Lafranchis *Marcoussis*. Paris, Les Editions du Temps, 1961

C. Zigrosser *The Complete Etchings of John Marin*. Philadelphia, Museum of Art, 1969

L. Saphire *André Masson: The Complete Graphic Work*, vol. i (1924–49). New York, Blue Moon Press, 1974

A. H. Barr, Jr. *Matisse, His Art and His Public*. New York, Museum of Modern Art, 1951

W. S. Lieberman, *Matisse, 50 Years of His Graphic Art*. New York, Braziller, 1956

C. Duthuit and M. Duthuit-Matisse

Henri Matisse: catalogue raisonné de l'œuvre gravé, vols. i and ii. Paris, Claude Duthuit, 1983

U. Schmitt Matta (Einführung und Katalog der druckgraphischen Werk im kunstmuseum Silkeborg). Silkeborg, Silkeborg Museum, 1969

R. Sabatier Matta: catalogue raisonné de l'œuvre gravé 1943–1974. Stockholm/Paris, Editions Sonet-Visat, 1975

P. Wember Joan Miró, das graphische Gesamtwerk. Krefeld, Kaiser Wilhelm Museum, 1957

F. Mourlot Joan Miró Lithographs, vol. i. New York, Tudor, 1972

J. Dupin Miró Graveur, vol. i, 1928–1960. Paris, Daniel Lelong Editeur, 1984

F. Mourlot Miró Lithographs, vol. ii, 1953–1963. Paris, Maeght Editeur, 1975

G. Cramer et al. Henry Moore, Catalog of Graphic Work, vol. i. Geneva, Cramer 1968, vol. ii, 1973

L. Vitali Giorgio Morandi: Opera Grafica. Turin, Einaudi 1957

S. Terenzio and D. C. Belknap The Prints of Robert Motherwell: A Catalogue Raisonné 1943–1984. New York, Hudson Hills Press, 1984

Otto Mueller, Das Graphische Gesamtwerk. Berlin, Galerie Nierendorf, 1974

S. Yanagi Shiko Munakata, Woodblock Prints. Tokyo, Chikuma-Shobo, 1958

G. Schiefler Verzeichnis des graphischen Werkes Edvard Munch bis 1906. Berlin, Cassirer, 1907

G. Schiefler Edvard Munch, Das graphische Werk 1906–1926. Berlin, Euphorion, 1927

W. Timm The Graphic Art of Edvard Munch. London, Studio Vista, 1969

J. Askelund The Graphic Art of Rolf Nesch. Detroit, Institute of Arts, 1969

U. Johnson Louise Nevelson Prints and Drawings, 1953–66. Brooklyn, The Brooklyn Museum, 1967

H. Davies and R. Castleman The Prints of Barnett Newman. New York, Barnett Newman Foundation, 1983

G. Schiefler Das graphische Werk Emil Noldes bis 1910. Berlin, Bard, 1911

G. Schiefler Das graphische Werk Emil Noldes 1910–1925. Berlin, Euphorion, 1926

G. Schiefler Das graphische Werk Emil Noldes, ed. C. Mosel, vols. i–ii. Cologne, Dumont Schauberg, 1966

Claes Oldenburg: Drawings, Watercolors and Prints. Stockholm, Moderna Museet, 1977

C. Orozco V. Catalogo Completo de la Obra Grafica de Orozco. San Juan, Marrozzini, [1970]

D. Kirkpatrick Eduardo Paolozzi. London, Studio Vista, 1971

R. Field The Lithographs and Etchings of Philip Pearlstein. Springfield, Missouri, Springfield Art Museum, 1978

P. Fechter Das graphische Werk Max Pechstein. Berlin, Gurlitt, 1921

U. Johnson Gabor Peterdi Graphics 1934–69. New York, Touchstone, [1970]

B. Geiser, Picasso Peintre-Graveur, vols. 1–2 (1899–1934). Vol. 1 published by author, 1933, vol. 2 published Bern, Kornfeld and Klipstein, 1968

F. Mourlot Picasso Lithographe, vols. 1–4 (1919–63). Monte Carlo, Sauret, 1949–64

W. Boeck Pablo Picasso Linolschnitte. Teufen, Niggli, 1962

G. Bloch Pablo Picasso, Catalogue of the Printed Graphic Work, vols. 1–2 (1904–69). Bern, Kornfeld and Klipstein, 1968–71

B. Baer Picasso peintre-graveur, vol. iii, 1935–45. Bern, Editions Kornfeld, 1986

P. Cramer Pablo Picasso: The Illustrated Books. Geneva, Patrick Cramer, 1983

F. V. O'Connor and E. V. Thaw Jackson Pollock: A Catalogue Raisonné of Prints, Drawings and Other Works. New Haven, Yale University Press, 1978

O. Breicha Arnulf Rainer, Überdeckungen

mit einem Werkkatalog sämtlicher Radierungen, Lithographien und Siebdrucke 1950–1971. Vienna, Edition Tusch, 1972

E. A. Foster Robert Rauschenberg Prints 1948–70. Minneapolis, Institute of Art, 1970

M. de la Motte Robert Rauschenberg. Hanover, Kestner-Gesellschaft, 1970

P. Vogt Christian Rohlfs, Œuvre-Katalog der Druckgraphik. n.p., 1950

James Rosenquist: Graphic Retrospective. Sarasota, Fla., John and Mable Ringling Museum of Art, 1979

Dieter Rot Books and Graphics 1947–71. London, The Arts Council, 1973

Dieter Rot Books and Graphics Part 1, 1947–1971. Stuttgart/London/Reykjavik, Edition Hansjörg Meyer, 1972; Part 2 and Other Stuff, 1979

I. and O. Rouault The Graphic Work of Rouault, vols. i and ii. Monaco, Editions André Sauret, 1978

M. Galfetti Antonio Saura, la obra grafica 1958–1984. Madrid, Ministerio de Cultura, 1985

R. Schapire Karl Schmidt-Rottluffs graphische Werk bis 1923. Berlin, Euphorion, 1924

E. Rathenau Karl Schmidt-Rottluff. Das graphische Werk seit 1923. New York, Rathenau, [1964]

G. Wietek Schmidt-Rottluff Graphik, Munich, Karl Thiemig, 1971

U. Johnson Karl Schrag the Graphic Works (1939–70). Syracuse, Syracuse University Press, 1971

A. Lioré and P. Cailler Catalogue de l'œuvre gravé de Dunoyer de Segonzac, vols. i–ii. Geneva, Cailler, 1958

R. Mason Kurt Seligmann, œuvre gravé. Geneva, Musée d'art et d'histoire, 1982

K. Prescott The Complete Graphic Works of Ben Shahn. New York, Quadrangle, 1973

P. Morse John Sloan's Prints. New Haven, Yale University Press, 1969

G. Duby Soulages, eaux-fortes, lithographies, 1952–1973. Paris, Yves Rivière, 1974

R. H. Axsom The Prints of Frank Stella: A Catalogue Raisonné 1967–1982. New York, Hudson Hills Press; Ann Arbor, Michigan Museum of Art, 1983

F. H. Man Graham Sutherland. Das graphische Werk. 1922–1970. Munich, Galerie Wolfgang Ketterer, [1970]

W. Hofmann 'Antoni Tàpies', Huitième Exposition Internationale de Gravure, 1969. Ljubljana, Moderna Galerija, 1969

V. Vasarely Vasarely, vols. 1–2. Neuchâtel, Editions du Griffon, 1967–70

J. Auberty and C. Perussaux Jacques Villon, catalogue de son œuvre gravé. Paris, Prouté, 1950

C. de Ginestet and C. Pouillon Jacques Villon, les estampes et les illustrations. Paris, Arts et Métiers Graphiques, 1979

K. von Walterskirchen Maurice de Vlaminck Verzeichnis des graphischen Werkes. Bern, Benteli, [1974]

R. Crone Andy Warhol. New York, Praeger; London, Thames and Hudson, 1970

F. Feldman and J. Schellmann Andy Warhol Prints. New York, Ronald Feldman Fine Arts and Abbeville Press; Munich, Editions Schellman, 1985

W. Grohmann 'Das graphische Werk von Wols' in Quadrum, VI (1959)

D. Brusberg Paul Wunderlich Werkverzeichnis der Lithografien von 1949–71. Berlin, Propyläen, 1971

Index

Figures in italic refer to monochrome illustrations, bold numerals to color plates

237